Also by Anthony Duncan:
 The Lord of the Dance

Forthcoming in this series:
 The Temple of the Spirit
 The Seventh Angel
 Recollections of a Green Man

GW00566615

The Sword in the Sun

dialogue with an angel

Anthony Duncan

SUN CHALICE

BOOKS

1997

Published by
SUN CHALICE BOOKS
PO Box 9703
Albuquerque, New Mexico
USA 87119

Publisher's Cataloging-in-publication Data
Duncan, Anthony
    The Sword in the Sun / Anthony Duncan
        p.   cm.
    1. Angels
2. Magic   3. Spiritual life   I. Title
BF1623.K55 D99   1997   133.4
ISBN 0-9650839-4-2

Cover design by Nicholas Whitehead

Contents

Author's Preface

This is the second of five books, written between the summer of 1971 and that of 1975, within the context of a profound inner compulsion. It is also, possibly, the most extraordinary.

It is less of a book than an experience. The experience was my own, over several weeks. The reader must make what he or she can of it and no doubt all manner of explanations and learned interpretations may be forthcoming!

The invitation is to overhear a series of conversations. After more than twenty years the memory of them is vivid and, for myself at any rate, endearing.

An eavesdropper is not one who is being lectured at or persuaded to adopt a particular viewpoint. He or she is entirely free of such constraints and can come and go as curiosity demands.

This book was written in Gloucestershire on either side of my forty-second birthday. It was perhaps easier to record such a conversation then than it might be now, at age sixty-five! I don't know; but I am personally profoundly grateful for it and for all its face-value implies.

It is important, however, for me to bear in mind that, as St. Gregory of Sinai reminds us, there are but three purposes for which men may put pen to paper without fault or constraint.

> The first as memoranda for themselves; the second, for the benefit of others; the third, for obedience. But he who writes to please men, for fame or for display, loses his reward and will receive no profit from this either here or in the life to come.

This book is offered, as it was written, in a spirit of obedience and in the sincere hope that there are others than its author who will derive benefit from it.

Corbridge, Northumberland. November 1995.

The Wheel of Life

The Wheel of Life

i

I was sitting at my desk in the study when I became aware of someone standing beside me, a little behind my left shoulder. The visitor was no stranger to me. We had enjoyed much conversation together in the past and he had taught me many things. He had spoken to me of Almighty God, and, over the years, he had brought me to an understanding of my own self. There was a most profound bond of love between us. I wondered what this visitation meant. I became silent. He spoke:

Angel: We have work to do together. It will not be easy. We must converse in order that others may overhear us and we must speak of deep and weighty matters. But we must also take good care that those who hear have no decisions made for them. They must think for themselves. Many of them will think you mad, my Brother, and you must be content to be mad in this life. And who knows? Mad you may be! But you are loved no less for that, and what else would you have but the Love of Christ?

Me: I love working with you. Life becomes full of surprises and everything and everybody becomes more lovable, more real. I know that 'knowledge' is of no great consequence of itself. It tends, as St. Paul said, to make us self-important and to imagine that we are somebody. But it is a very lovely and a wonderful thing for mortal man to hear of God and of the things of God, as long as we learn to love the more because of it.

I am fearful — I make no bones about it — I do not relish the thought of being overheard. It will do my standing no good among my fellow-clergymen. 'What?' they will say, 'a clergy-man talking to an angel? Haven't the scholars explained angels away? And fancy being overheard! Bad form, that! And who does he want us to think he is?' I think I am being honest when I say that I would rather be thought mad than presumptuous, but I am not sufficiently sure of my own motives to be certain about any of them.

Angel: Does any of this matter? Do I show you the things of God for your own private entertainment? And what nonsense you talk about your brethren. Do they not know you, with all your failings? Are you not projecting upon them your own reaction: jealousy and spiritual pride? And who cares about human scholarship? Do I cease to exist because some clever fellow has abolished me? Let us care for the integrity of the scholar and take his scholarship as we find it. And what is all this talk about honesty? The one true word you uttered concerned your ignorance of any of your motives. Have I not labored these forty years and more to show you yourself, and you begin this work of ours together by blowing up a great balloon and painting your own face upon it. Behold, little Brother, I have a pin!

Me: Thank God for your pin! Now I have talked my nonsense and slandered my brethren, and reminded myself of my own frailty, please God we may proceed. You know me too well. I cannot deceive you and you will not let me deceive myself. To my slandered brethren, I apologize! You were so right; I projected myself upon them. I erected a great defensive work about me. Thank you for demolishing it so kindly.

Angel: The End is coming, the time is growing short. There are many matters which have been unimportant until now, but which now become important, for a New Age is in process of coming to birth and the way must be prepared in advance of it. Mortal man is fallible and possesses little objectivity. This much you have demonstrated at the outset, and it is as well that you did so. The opinions of men are of more importance to mortal man than God's truth. This must be recognized at the outset and firmly set aside thereafter. All men are redeemed, yet in this world all are fallen.

Me: The End? The Second Coming? I wonder if any of us take this seriously? It was the central hope of the early Church. Two things only mattered to them: the Resurrection and the Second Coming. These two great realities were what the Faith was all about. And now we half-deny the first and disbelieve the second. I don't think we even want our Lord to come again. I think we want everybody to go to Church on Sundays and live good, kindly and compassionate lives, and all go to 'heaven' when they die, with no wars, no civil commotions, no troubles and nothing out of place for ever and ever, Amen! The Second Coming? We don't want one. And all men redeemed? Only if they say their prayers and go to Church like good boys and girls. It wouldn't be fair on the good people if the bad ones went to heaven as well. Now then, my dear angelic Brother, isn't this the way we are? Tell me I am wrong, for what a horrid thing I have just described.

Angel: Does it matter if you take it seriously or not? Will that make any difference to the End when it comes about? Will our Lord delay his Coming Again to await the good pleasure of his Bishops or of that hotchpotch of man-made institutions that they call 'the Church?' Bless them all! Yes, and they are blessed. Is the Creator of Heaven and earth to be constrained? You take yourselves too seriously, mortal men.

Me: Are you telling me that right belief does not matter? Or that ultimate things are so inexorable that it matters not at all how men react, what they believe, how they behave or anything they do? Is a man to be redeemed against his will? Where is free will then? Where is the image of God in him? Where is man himself? And for my own part, why have I tried so hard not to fall into that which I know to be sin — although Heaven knows, and you know, how often I have fallen? Call me foolish if you will, but is a man to be redeemed against his own better judgment?

Angel: Am I to do your thinking for you? Use your better judgment, Brother.

Me: I had expected more than that. The silence is disconcerting. And you will have me answer my own questions? Very well then. Right belief matters very much, but it is subordinate to the loving and obedient response of a human soul to our Lord's outstretched hand. We can never, in this life, fully understand the Mysteries of the Incarnation, but it is we ourselves who are injured by distorted beliefs and not the Truth itself. We diminish our own fulfillment, our joy, our humanity, by our wrong beliefs. But we are not rejected because of them. We are loved too much for that. Right belief, orthodox theology, matters exceedingly for Truth's sake, and for our humanity's sake; but Love matters even more. How is that for a start?

Angel: Very well. Now continue.

Me: You make me work hard. Ultimate things are inexorable in that there are cycles which have their correspondence in human time scales. There is free-will, but there is not unlimited time to use it. A man's response to our Lord is not just crying 'Lord, Lord!' It is expressed in 'doing the Father's will.' So my weak efforts to keep out of sin are a part of my response. It is a *continuing* response of Love, while time lasts for me.

Angel: Well done! It is the whole tenor of a life that matters; this *is* the human response. Your response is renewed every day, and all day long. Continue.

Me: Is a man to be redeemed against his will? What of the man whose whole life is a rejection of our Lord? I do not mean a rejection through ignorance, I mean a freely willed refusal of redemption, either by conscious declaration or by the whole tenor of life. At the End, what then? The idea of Universal Salvation, willy nilly, seems somehow immoral; and yet the idea of eternal damnation, or extinction, seems a defeat of Love. I cannot come to any satisfactory conclusions about this, unaided.

Angel: There is more to this than you suppose. In a sense you may say that *both* Universal Salvation *and* the destruction of the self-damned are parts of the same great Truth. The two concepts seem as irreconcilable as they are unimaginable to your mortal mind. But their identity is a simple matter as I shall show you in a little while. You have not answered all your questions, and in your answers you have raised even more questions! (But we must leave something for those who are listening to us to get their teeth into. We must not do their thinking for them.)

The Sword in the Sun

ii

The following day, the angel came again; but it would be more truthful to say that I became aware of his presence, for as I well know, he is always present with me. Once more, he spoke:

Angel: I am glad you have written that I am always with you, for as you know, I am your Guardian Angel.

Me: I very well remember the occasion when you first showed yourself to me. I was making my thanksgivings after offering the Eucharist, when suddenly, you were there! I saw you with an inner vision; a man-like shape, apparently made of a bright, copper-colored flame. The overwhelming impression I received was of a quite unfathomable love, and directed, of all persons, to me! I fear my description is a poor one and unflattering.

Angel: You saw me as I am! The previous day your consciousness was raised in prayer until you found yourself in the presence of many angels and of discarnate human souls. Do you remember both the sense of copper-colored flame and of beings robed in white? The images of heaven in holy Scripture have become debased in the minds of mortal men, but their reality is unaffected, as all mortal men shall shortly discover.

Me: I have asked this question before, but because we are to be overheard I will ask it again. Has every human being in this world his own personal Guardian Angel?

Angel: No. But all have guardians of a sort. Most are human guardians, human souls with whom they are eternally associated. Some have guardians from among the angels. It all depends upon the needs of each and every individual soul. There is no idea of rank or merit; every guardian partakes of the Mind of Christ, and loves his charge with the Love of Christ.

Me: Then the term 'guardian angel' may mean, for us, either a human or an angelic being. Either may fulfill that office. Tell me, does this office ever fail?

Angel: Never! But your free will is forever inviolate. You can make yourself impossible to guard. Your integrity is the key to all things.

Me: Tell me, if you will, the difference between angels and men. I read somewhere that the great theologian, Origen, thought they were the same beings. Other theologians think 'angels' in the Scriptures are mere literary devices, or names for divinely given intuitions.

Angel: You and your theologians! It is as well for us all that our Lord cares nothing for theology. Origen was mistaken. Angels and men belong to wholly different orders of creation. First the angels were created, and then Man. And we are happy to serve our little Brothers. Notice: I am your guardian, you are not mine.

Me: 'I am among you as he that serveth.' In a topsy-turvy world normality itself seems upside down, and the idea of the greater serving the lesser is one which we find hard to grasp. And yet the best of human leaders spend themselves in service to their subordinates. I am about to talk nonsense; guard me, my Brother!

Angel: Men have not always had angel guardians. This is a fruit of the Incarnation. Before our Lord's Resurrection, men had no guardians at all, either human or angelic. This guardianship is a temporary thing. At the end of the age it will cease; after then it will no longer be needed.

The Wheel of Life

Me: Then we are in an age of transition? Guardianship, angelic or human, belongs to the period between our Lord's Incarnation and his Coming Again? What happens then? What happens to this world? Will it be destroyed? Does the whole of Creation undergo a catastrophic change?

Angel: You ask too many questions at once! Why are you so concerned about the world at the Second Coming? You are doing your very best to destroy it yourselves, and yourselves with it. Why this sudden concern? Does God love the world even less than you do?

Me: I think we love ourselves, and love the world only because we identify it with ourselves. We will exploit it, but we fear to lose it. I think we are remarkably stupid. A moment's thought is enough to show us how we should conduct ourselves — but we cannot behave even if we have thought about it. I blame the Fall! But I am, in part at least, responsible for the Fall, and it is no good blaming the past all the time. We talk too much about the Fall, and yet... its effects are manifest. I think we are in a bad way.

Angel: What do you know about the Fall? Your mythology gives expression to what your folk-memory remembers; but the memories are vague. You only know the effects; you can only guess the cause. The whole truth of the Fall is altogether beyond your knowing. You are right, you talk too much of the Fall. St. Paul never intended Adam and Eve to be so obsessively rediscovered! You are redeemed; your frailty is made a means of Grace. Forget the Fall. You are to live the Risen Life, and in this age of transition your guardians are there to help you. This very age, terrible though it is, is itself a means of Grace as you shall discover.

Here, our conversation came to an end. I had asked a lot of questions, and had both questions and answers in reply. You who read this, ask your own questions and take nothing as proven until it is true for you. The age of dogmatism is past.

The Sword in the Sun

iii

Angel: It is time we introduced a third party. Here is Pan!

Me: Pan? Does he really exist? Who is he? What am I to make of him?

Angel: Pan is the hierarch of the Elemental creatures on earth. If you like, you may call him the King of the Fairies. Like me, he is your Brother in Christ.

Me: You said that men would call me mad! I believe you, as you know, but what of all those who may overhear our conversation?

Angel: Does any of this matter? Men must make up their own minds. Are we to do their thinking for them?

Pan: I am standing by your right shoulder. I have come in from the garden.

Me: Do you live in the garden? Where? What do you do?

Pan: I live everywhere on earth. My children live in your garden. The garden is full of them.

Me: Why can't I see them? I can feel their presence sometimes. I have been taught to sense them, and to sense the life in trees and flowers, and in rocks and hills too. Why can't I see you or your children?

Pan: We don't live in this world in the same way that you do. We live in this world as it really is. You live in it in a strange way we cannot understand.

Me: Is this house real to you? Are our roads and railways and factories and cities real to you? Are we driving you out and making life difficult for you? What can we do to become more aware of you? We must do you terrible mischief. I am sorry.

Pan: You cannot understand. Your house is here, and then again, it is not here. It is not in our world, but we are in both worlds. This must seem very difficult for you.

Me: Yes, very difficult! But in some strange way I can understand. It is as if we live on two different wavelengths in the same world; different, but close to one another. If my house is not in your world, what is here in its place? And what about me? Where am I if I am not here in your world?

Pan: You ask too many questions; I do not know all the answers! As to your house; in your world it is here, in my world we are in the middle of a lake. My world is nicer. And you? You are in both, and yet not in both. I cannot explain. Let us leave you in your house, it is easier that way.

Angel: You are right about the wavelengths. Pan does not know these things because they are not his concern. And you shall not know how it is that you are in both worlds at once until the End.

Me: But what of our misuse of this world, our spoiling of it, our pollution of its atmosphere, the sea and everything else? Do we harm the Elementals or their world? We play havoc with the plants. What of the animals? How much damage can we do?

Angel: You cannot do as much damage as you think, and you are paying for that which you have done. I will not elaborate, but meditate upon the sorrows of your world of men. Are you happy in your cities? Do you enjoy your riches? And is war a truly entertaining pastime? You harm the Devas of your world; you harm the animals that belong to your world and the harm rebounds upon your own head. But no harm is permanent, and all is passing and shall soon be past.

Me: Who are the Devas? You have told me, but I would hear it again.

Angel: Hear their King! He will tell you.

Pan: They are the spirits of wood and water, field and tree, and plant and stone.

Me: Are they the same as the Fairies, or are they of another order? And are you their King too?

Pan: They are of another order, but they are my children. This world of nature is my Kingdom under Christ.

Me: Then what am I doing here? What is our relationship? And what, please tell me, of the animals?

Angel: Pan does not know the answers to these questions. He lives ever in the present moment for this is the nature of Eternity. You men came here by the Fall, and your world evolved to catch you as you fell. Pan is your Brother in Christ, and you are King of the animals in your world. The plants belong to Pan.

Me: What a horror for the animals! And what an outrage on a royal Brother! What restitution can I make?

Angel: Your restitution is your own unhappiness. All judgments in Eternity are self-inflicted. You exact revenge upon your own self. There is no escape; but have no fear, you are redeemed.

Me: What can I do, if not to make amends, yet to befriend a Brother? How do I conduct myself to Pan?

Angel: Acknowledge that he *is*. And you will find the whole world come alive before your eyes. You will have begun within yourself a cure for your own blindness, and when next you pluck a flower, it will be 'by your leave!' Courtesy is the hallmark of Heaven!

Me: Then Pan, my Brother, I acknowledge you and all your children. And I ask your pardon for my trespass. And I trust that we may come to glorify God in partnership and rid the world of man-made sorrows.

Pan: I am well pleased! And now I go about my world. Call me, Brother, when you will, for I am everywhere to be found.

Angel: And that will do for one day's work. All you who overhear, take note! But do not take too much at once; just think it possible that the conversation was real.

iv

Angel: It is time we spoke about life itself. Where did you come from, little Brother? Where were you before you were born; before you were even conceived? Answer me that if you dare!

Me: If I dare? You put me in a very vulnerable position. I once thought that I was created by God at my conception and had no existence before. I imagined that Holy Church required me to think this and that if I speculated much on this matter I would be in danger of straying from Christian Orthodoxy. But I will be bold: I *was* before I was born.

Angel: My brave fellow! And what is this orthodoxy which forbids you to think? Is it so jealous in defense of Almighty God that it fears you will unseat him with your much thinking? And how can truth be at variance with Truth? You have ever been and ever shall be, and have lived on earth since your fall many, many times.

Me: Now we are in trouble, you and I. This is the doctrine of Reincarnation, and no orthodox Christian can admit such a doctrine. It denies the objectivity of Baptism; it denies the doctrine of Redemption, and it plays havoc with the Resurrection! We have strayed from orthodoxy, Brother; and you an angel!

Angel: What nonsense is this? Will you ever limit Almighty God and make a theologian of him? If your understanding of these things is as vulnerable as that, they were almost too flimsy to save you. You have dug a trench and hidden within it for fear some other calls you heretic.

Me: You are quite right, I will not deny it for a moment. But is this doctrine of reincarnation important? Why did our Lord say nothing of it? Why no reference — no clear reference at any rate — in holy Scripture?

Angel: No, it is not important. It would have clouded the issues with which our Lord dealt in his Incarnate Life. But look: the Jews were almost all alone in having no such doctrine. Why?

Me: You ask me? But indeed I remember that you once told me and I will put it as simply as I can. The rest of mankind had a *static* concept of creation, and their doctrine of reincarnation was a kind of 'wheel of life,' forever turning, but going nowhere. The aim of man was to so destroy his own senses that he remained forever at the 'hub' with no independent existence. The Jews were given a sense of *process*; theirs was a *dynamic* concept of creation. Things were in motion, history was significant, there would be an end product to things. An awareness of reincarnation would have confused them utterly and a whole dimension of human understanding would have been lost. But I suppose the static and the dynamic ideas are not as contradictory as they seem. In all probability you will tell me that they are complementary — at least as far as mortal man's understanding is concerned.

Angel: In all probability I shall. Well done! You learned your lesson well.

Me: But come now. Are we to leave the matter there? What about the reconciliation of the idea of reincarnation with the objectivity of Baptism, of Redemption, of the Resurrection? We are being overheard!

Angel: Then let our eavesdroppers think for themselves. Come, Brethren, think: Why should these things be at variance? And do not look over your shoulders to see who is watching you. Think! And if you stay with us — who knows? — you may hear the answers given.

V

Angel: The Wheel of Life goes round and round. Comment upon that, little Brother!

Me: It depends upon what you mean. If you mean that, as the Hindus and Buddhists believe, things just go on and on with neither progress nor purpose, I think it is a pretty uninspiring idea. I don't believe it! Comment, dear Brother!

Angel: Neither do I believe it. Yet, in a sense it is so. And do not be so hasty to generalize about the beliefs of Hindus and Buddhists. They may not recognize themselves from your description.

Me: Very well, then, I accept that all things are eternal in that they abide within the eternal Mind of God and are loved with an everlasting Love. I accept that the whole of Creation is, as it were, a Great Dance, with our Lord the Christ in the midst as Lord of the Dance. You have told me of that, at length. But is there no *progress*? Is the whole business not too much like a merry-go-round if we cannot see a *process* at work? Does the whole of Creation just go round and round, twinkling prettily, until the Almighty tires of it, and the music stops? Surely not! This would not be child-*like*, it would be rather child-*ish*, and that is by no means the same thing.

Angel: If you only knew how prettily you twinkle! Why should there be any difficulty in reconciling the static and the dynamic? All things *are,* eternally. And living things live; their lives are cyclic; every measure of the Dance is different. Mortal men are quickly bored because no earthly thing can satisfy them. I assure you, there is no tedium in Heaven!

Me: Now you will be telling me that I am confusing the hopeless sense of 'no progress' of the primitive Eastern idea of reincarnation with a Creation which is static in its *abiding*, but dynamic in its *living*. I have emerged from that confusion now, have I not?

Angel: You have. And let us defer our discussion of reincarnation until some other time. Our eavesdroppers will attach too much importance to it if they hear too much at once.

Me: Communists lose patience with Christians and adherents of other religions, in that they accuse us of looking for a fulfillment in some other world and neglecting the perfection of this one. I do not care for their idea of perfection, but there is some justice in their complaint.

Angel: You have not finished. You have something in mind. Go on!

Me: Yes, I am thinking of a little graph that Pierre Teilhard de Chardin drew in *The Future of Man*. The aspiration of the Communist was horizontal — the horizontal coordinate; and that of the Christian was the vertical coordinate.

Angel: And he reconciled the two by drawing a line at an angle of forty-five degrees, thereby meeting both requirements! Yes indeed, but there is more to it than that.

Me: Yes, he recognized the possibility that there would have to be an evolution of this world before 'Omega.'

Angel: Please define 'Omega' for me.

Me: I had hoped that you would do that for me! Very well then. It is the Second Coming, the dawn of a totally new age, the fulfillment of the process that has been going on in and among men. Teilhard, I think, conceived it as the culmination of the process of evolution — man evolved from the hydrogen atom — and now this process turning inwards upon itself to arrive at its plenitude. But words are just words! Omega is the 'End' — the end product of things.

Angel: What things?

Me: You are determined to make me work! Omega is the fulfillment of many things — at least this is how I understand it. First, it is the fulfillment of that whole process of evolution which produced this creature called 'man' in this world. Man, if Teilhard is right, is the fulfillment of consciousness in *matter* — in the world, this wavelength, call it what you will, in which mortal men abide. A process has been going on; we call it evolution. Omega is the end product — the fulfillment of the process.

But this is not all. Omega is the fulfillment of another process, the process of redemption. Somehow, in some way, man fell from Grace, and the Lord became incarnate into the world of mortal men, identified it with Himself, and we are now in the transitional period before that process of redemption is fulfilled. Omega is the moment of fulfillment.

Angel: Well done! Now reconcile for me the process of the evolution of mortal man and the undoubted reality of an historical fall.

Me: Do I burst into song? Poetry can express this; mythology can express it. History and theology are hard pressed, I think.

Angel: Do I ask for theology? What myths have you in mind?

Me: Adam and Eve in the Garden of Eden. And the myths concerning Atlantis and Lemuria. The Australian Aborigines talk of the 'Dream Time,' and there is the myth of Noah and the Flood.

Angel: What have these in common?

Me: I cannot speak for the 'Dream Time' myths because I don't know enough about them, but all the others speak of catastrophe to man through the weight of human sin. And sin is rebellion against God — seeking to be one's own god. Furthermore, all the myths have at once a convincing and yet unreal quality. They are true, and yet they can't have happened as historical events — not in our *kind* of history at any rate. The story of Noah might be a folk memory of floods at the end of the last Ice Age, but it doesn't feel like one. Not to me.

Angel: All these things are parts of the same folk-memory. When man fell, he fell from one wavelength into another. These are memories of another world. That is why they will not relate to this one. And they find echoes in this world which only serve to make confusion worse confounded.

Me: You spoke of the evolution of this wavelength being prepared for men to 'fall into.' Did men fall into identification with an innocent, Paleolithic cave-man? Is this what those odd first four verses of the sixth chapter of Genesis are trying to say? And by this fall we become identified with the whole of animal life which has evolved for our salvation?

Angel: Yes. I have spoken of this before and you remember well. Teilhard was right to see man's evolution turning in upon itself. This began when man identified with Paleolithic earthly man. This was the dawn of reflection upon this wavelength, of objectivity in consciousness. It was a marriage of two quite different creatures. One was destroyed; its being lost, its consciousness identified with another creature altogether. Hence the tension in you, mortal man! But all is well! In Christ's incarnation you are all new-made. He has identified you with Himself, and all of Heaven is topsy-turvy. Did I not tell you that we know no tedium?

30

Me: I am exhausted. I must take a little while to grasp the measure of things. I had not realized that I was once destroyed, and given being again by identification with a creature of a lower order. I was never angel then?

Angel: Nor I ever man. Man was, and is, and is to come. But many things have happened on the way. Now let us leave our hearers to make what they will of what they have overheard.

The Sword in the Sun

vi

Angel: It is time we spoke of prayer. Why are you so shy of speaking about your prayers?

Me: I suspect that it is because I fear lest I seem to be making something of myself. This is a temperamental thing I suppose. Not just my own temperament, but an inhibition that I share with others. And prayer is an intensely private thing; yet I acknowledge that it is something 'given,' and what is given is given for the benefit of others.

Angel: I abide forever, fully conscious, in the Mind and Presence of God my Creator. Am I shy of saying so? And shy of whom?

Me: Very well then. I renounce all reticence. I would share your conscious abiding, forever. What else do I want?

Angel: If you want nothing else, then you shall have what you desire. Now tell me of your prayers.

Me: I started to 'say my prayers' when I was fifteen. I had never been taught. My family was alienated from the Institutional Church.

Angel: They were alienated from great humbug and false religion, and saved their integrity thereby. Have no fears for them; they are safe indeed. Continue.

The Sword in the Sun

Me: When I was twenty-four, a subaltern in the British Army of the Rhine I spent a week-end at a Chaplains' Department house in Verden. There, I had a terrible and most wonderful experience.

Angel: Tell me all about it. Conceal nothing. I was there.

Me: The Chaplain had been reading from C.S. Lewis' book, *The Screwtape Letters*. I was much impressed and borrowed it to read that night in bed. As I read, I realized that I was reading about myself. My awful sinfulness became apparent to me, and at last I could stand it no longer. I fell on my knees on the floor. I cannot remember if I said anything. I only knew myself as I really was — hideous and lost! Brother; finish the story for me, if you will.

Angel: You saw a light when everything was darkness. You knew yourself forgiven and experienced a Peace which was, to you, unfathomable. I spoke to you and put the inner message into words. You made your confession the following day, and the day after that was the Feast of the Transfiguration.

Me: What was it that I went through? How do I describe such an experience? There are so many different names for things.

Angel: Some call it 'sensible conversion.' It was a mystical experience of great profundity. You lived again your own destruction; it was a self-inflicted sentence. And then you lived again your re-creation, and the light you saw was the Christ Himself who made you and redeemed you.

Me: I was married, and was standing in Church in Singapore, singing the *Magnificat* at Evensong on Easter Day. Suddenly, between one verse and another, something happened. I knew then that I must leave the Army and become a priest.

Angel: I was allowed to interpose and take your consciousness to a higher level, and you received from the lips of Christ his will for you. It took you long enough to do it !

Me: Did I drag my feet? The thought of it appalled me, and so much was in the way. Did I delay unnecessarily?

Angel: Not in time, but a little in will. Yet all is well and you are forgiven for that. Indeed for all that was, and is and shall be, you are forgiven!

Me: How can I be forgiven for what shall be? Is this a kind of blank check to sin? I know it is not, but please explain.

Angel: Forgiveness *is*. You abide in an ambience of forgiveness and restoration. If you love, you will not sin; and if you sin and seek forgiveness for love's sake, then it is all about you. But you will not escape the earthly consequences of your sin, as well you know.

Me: There is a lot to take in here. There is a multitude of questions which clamor to be asked. But they are too many, and their answering will take too long. And many will be answered in the mere asking of them. What would you have me do?

Angel: What you will. We shall return to prayer now we have overcome your reticence. There is much reticence to deal with yet, however!

Me: You terrify me! I can think of many things that I have learned to speak about to you, but could not mention to another man for sheer embarrassment and shame. Remember; we are overheard!

Angel: Enough for now. All things have their place, and in their place there is no place for shame.

Me: Then we shall leave our hearers wondering. But in their wondering, I hope they will remember that forgiveness *is*, and that those things locked deep within their hearts are shared with others far more widely than they know.

The Sword in the Sun

vii

Angel: The Wheel of Life; let us return to this.

Me: I do not know what to make of it. I have a mental image of a wheel mounted horizontally, turning like a merry-go-round.

Angel: Put the seasons of the year upon it. See how they change.

Me: Spring, Summer, Autumn, Winter. And then begin again. And on it goes, over and over again. And the plants conform to it. 'Seedtime and harvest shall not fail,' said God to Noah. Is this what you mean?

Angel: Yes. Now put your own life upon it. See where it goes.

Me: Conception, birth, growth, decline, death. What then?

Angel: Rebirth of course, what else? But do not worry, there is more to it than this. I am not telling you a tale of reincarnation as you think I am. Reincarnation is a fact, but it is a fact of Love and not of Law. The Law was fulfilled at the Incarnation, and men have passed from Law to Love. Baptism is the gate to Life for every man, and once through that gate, he comes and goes as Love alone decides. The Wheel of Life is driven by Love.

Me: And so we come into this world to be Baptized, and once Baptized, need never come again?

Angel: Need never come! Yet nearly all do come, once or often, to realize that which has been freely given them.

Me: And do they come back Christian? Is a man Baptized over and over again?

Angel: Sometimes, and sometimes not! Where is your problem?

Me: If I was Baptized last time, why was I Baptized this time?

Angel: How do you know if you were Baptized before? And how do you know that all your Hindus and Buddhists did not receive the Sacrament in ancient Rome, or if you like, Byzantium? Perhaps Love demands that they experience a truth outside the Christian consciousness in earthly life. How do you know? And does it matter to you if Love alone determines it?

Me: But what about the Mission Field? Are we not to preach the Gospel to every creature? Am I not inhibited if I wonder if a heathen pygmy is a former Pope?

Angel: Just do as you are told for Love's sake. The Lord will send you whom he will. The process is all but complete, yet many, many souls remain. This is no time for dragging feet.

Me: But does this not make nonsense of theology?

Angel: Only if the theology is too small to compass it. Our Lord is not too small, and Heaven is big enough. Why do you fear if Love alone determines it? You little understand just how eternally objective Baptism is.

Me: But the Resurrection of the Body. Which body: pygmy or Pope?

Angel: Both, unless perchance they make the pygmy Pope! The Body of the Resurrection has many suits in its eternal wardrobe. Would you limit to a single life your own eternal potency? You are a Christian, not a Pharisee! You shall transcend all planes of being, and may come and go at will, wearing the suit that Love alone shall choose. It shall become you well!

Me: Am I man or woman? Am I both? Are there pretty dresses in my wardrobe?

Angel: You and I unite within ourselves both masculine and feminine polarities. Yet on your wavelength, polarities are at their most external, and you must be man or woman in your mortal life.

Me: Now I understand our Lord's remarks on marriage to the Sadducees. And in Heaven, we are androgyne?

Angel: Yes, but not at once. Polarity remains respected in the lower planes of Heaven. But that will do for one day's talk. Our hearers are perplexed enough.

The Sword in the Sun

viii

Angel: The Wheel of Life again. Who shall we put upon it now?

Me: Yourself, dear Brother. Or is that not appropriate?

Angel: Indeed it is; but you cannot understand its working in the angelic order. It is a matter of Light and Mind, and do not build your theories upon these two words, for you can have no knowledge of their meaning for us. Try again.

Me: Is it good manners to apply it to Pan? And to his children the Elementals and the Devas?

Angel: Ask him; he is by your side.

Me: Pan, my Brother, what of the Wheel of Life? How does it affect you? What does it mean to you?

Pan: It is my Joy! It is the very spice of Life!

Me: But you yourself; do birth and death affect you? And your children? What of them?

Pan: I do not understand the words. I only know the Joy of change, and change, and changelessness.

Me: But do your Elementals never die? Do they grow old? Are they born?

Pan: Am I an animal? No, they change, and change, and then they are young again. Or they are old.

Me: I am bewildered! But I begin to see how it is with you. And what a joy it is!

Angel: Pan does not understand the circumstances of man. It is not his concern. The Wheel of Life applies to every order of existence differently. It is not the mechanistic horror you imagine!

Me: How many orders of existence are there? Or is that an unanswerable question? How many orders of living beings are there? Is that a more sensible question to ask?

Angel: Yes, and still impossible to answer. Wait, little Brother, for the fullness of Heaven. You will find all things in the eyes of Christ.

Pan: I am, in this planet. Transcendent and Immanent, an image of my Maker. My children are within me, and I am everywhere with them.

Me: Did you create your children, Pan? And you yourself created. How did you come to receive them all. And are there any lost?

Pan: I cannot remember; things were ever so. I do not ask such questions for I do not need the answers.

Angel: All life is the gift of Life Himself. All is gift, all is given. We build from what is given us; our raw material is Love. Sometimes you call it 'energy.' Love is a better word.

Me: May I ask, dear Brother Pan, how much you know, and what is the limit of your knowing? Forgive me, is this impertinent?

Pan: I know no limits. I know by wanting to know, and what I do not want to know, I know not.

Angel: Pan only knows that which concerns him. He has no need of other knowledge, and therefore he does not seek it. Heaven is very simple; there are no examinations!

Me: I think the pair of you are laughing at me. But not unkindly. I begin to laugh at myself with you. I am glad I am not a theologian; I should be in terrible confusion.

Angel: Then your duty would be plain: to pray and use your gift of reason to reconcile all difficulties with the Revelation given you in Christ. Do not misunderstand my speaking lightly of theology. It is the rational expression of what has been Revealed. Its concern is God's Truth. And who told you that you are no theologian? Have you not written learned books, crammed full of your theology?

Me: I stand corrected! You speak lightly of mere human cleverness, such as St. Paul referred to. I hope I speak lightly of the same.

Pan: I speak of wind and water, tree and stone. They are my children under Christ. They speak to me of the Love that gave them to me. That is my theology, little Brother.

Me: I want no better! Yet I am called to greater complication. Though if this be curse or blessing I can hardly say.

Angel: Curse it is; but out of curse comes blessing. Thank your Lord for that. Pan has much to teach you and you have much to learn. Learn from him, little Brother, and he will teach you to live in this world. For you shall have much to do with both it and him hereafter.

Me: What do you mean, hereafter? Do you mean when this mortal life is past, or do you mean in the age beyond the End?

Angel: The age beyond the End. Now you have it! O Brother, look to that age, for it is almost upon you.

Me: This is what I am waiting for. The age beyond Omega, when I shall abide consciously in the Mind and Presence of Christ, and come and go with you and Pan as Love alone determines. I would be pure in heart that I might see God.

Angel: If you would, you shall be. All shall have their desires; not all shall like them when they have them.

Pan: I do not know desire. I am, and my children are, and we are in Christ. I return to my children. Call me, Brother, I am everywhere in this world.

Me: Wind on the Wheel of Life, my Brothers I can hardly drive it fast enough. And yet, say 'death,' and I shall drag my feet like any other man. It will not do, I fear, to wish this life away before its every moment is fulfilled.

Angel: We have given our guests some thoughts to think. They must pick and choose and find the ones that fit. We will do no man's thinking for him. All decisions rest in the hands of those whose duty it is to make them. Take of what you have overheard if it rings true to you. And if it help you love your God and love your fellow-men the more, then hold to it; for this is the criterion.

The Evolution of Consciousness

i

Angel: We must move on to another dimension. Tell me all about the evolution of consciousness.

Me: Almost, I wish my name were Teilhard de Chardin. He has been my teacher, through his books.

Angel: And he himself was taught. What has he taught you?

Me: That in the Universe as we know it — on our wavelength of it, if you like — a process of evolution has been going on. This process has manifested two characteristics. The first is an ever increasing *complexity* of structure. Thus we see hydrogen atoms coalescing into gas-clouds and, we can only suppose by mutual attraction, compressing into great galaxies of stars and heating up until, in the conditions generated, the very atoms themselves become more complicated.

From here, we discover our Solar System: a star with satellites. Many different theories are advanced as to the origins of the system. Indeed there are many different theories about the origins of the Universe, but it appears to us that a cosmic catastrophe brought the planetary group into being — some say the explosion of a twin star of the Sun. If we confine our attention to Earth, we find a mass which is vastly more complex than the Sun. In time, the conditions are established for life to manifest, probably as single-cell organisms on the sea-bed. From there, plant and animal life developed. And each development involved a *compression* and a vast increase in *complexity*. The final, most developed, most complex creature is Man.

The second characteristic is the emergence of ever-higher degrees of *consciousness*. Consciousness is inherent in the hydrogen atom. The potential of the consciousness of matter is realized in the evolution of man who is the most complex creature. Complexity and consciousness seem, therefore, to be connected. Will this do as an exposition of evolution in a nutshell?

Angel: Admirably. Well done! But this is, as you have observed, a process upon one wavelength only. It is one dimension of many, and it is a man's eye view of it. You do not know, for example, what the Sun is.

Me: No. And you tempt me, I think, to mention something for which I feel an aversion. Many friends of mine, occultists and esotericists of various sorts, speak of a being called a 'Solar Logos,' as if the Sun itself, worshipped as a god in ancient Egypt, was in some sense a deity. I may misunderstand them, but some would, I think, identify it in some way with the Christ.

Angel: Why not? When the Christ has identified you with Himself. I think you are busy defending Almighty God again. Fear not, he will survive!

Me: Very well then, I will ask you directly. What is the Sun? What, if anything, do we understand by the 'Solar Logos?' And if there was a twin star — if the Sun was once a part of a binary system as some astronomers think — what was it? And what has become of it?

Angel: Are you holding your breath? Relax, little Brother! You ask me, 'what is the Sun?' You would not understand if I told you. But know that it is not unconnected with the angelic order. You ask me of the 'Solar Logos,' and I find the term extraordinary. There is much human guesswork, both on earth and in the lower planes of Heaven, about the angelic hierarchy. You mortal men love hierarchies! Most human souls who seek to communicate with mortal men through mediumship of various kinds are bubbling over with newfound joys which they do not yet begin to understand. When their understanding grows, they become less anxious to teach.

Me: A host of questions now. And which to ask first! The Church has frowned on mediumship; has she been wrong?

Angel: Yes and no. You believe in the Communion of Saints, but you will not practice it. And yet it would be a bad thing to depend too much on excitements and the *joie de vivre* of those newly arrived in Heaven. Few have anything to say, and all have better things to do. And so it was of her wisdom that the Church discouraged the use of these gifts. But, alas! It is not easy to strike a proper balance, and she has driven the gifted into dark corners, and the Grace of discernment of spirits has well-nigh perished by neglect. Without this Grace, the gifts can be dangerous indeed.

Me: Why? Oh! I know they can, but tell me why.

Angel: Let us talk of mediumship first. The medium can receive from three sources. The first is a human source from the lower planes of Heaven. The second is an etheric 'thought form' of human generation, and the third is a demonic source through the human faculties of a lost soul.

In the case of the first, the source is honest but ignorant. Normal critical criteria must always apply to anything received, for life on the lower planes of heaven is largely subjective and has been aptly described as 'ideo-plastic.' This is an entertaining word. Bear it in mind.

In the case of the second, the thought-form has been constructed by mortal men in their collective imagination; sometimes by an individual imagination. And it will transmit, very faithfully, the collective doctrines and concepts with which it has been identified. It has a measure of autonomous existence largely, but not entirely, maintained from the collective energies of those who have constructed it. Such were most of the heathen 'gods.' They were not evil in themselves, they were merely made in man's image!

I will not dwell on the third case here. It is sufficient that the possibility exists. Mediumship, you will observe, is a human-to-human phenomenon.

Me: I am alarmed about the 'thought forms!' It makes sense of a great deal of what I had imagined was nonsense, and I have read of this possibility before. Can they be vehicles for demonic use?

Angel: Let us not concern ourselves with demons. Yes, the possibility exists, but it is rare. Consider, however, the spectacle of earnest mortal men and women sitting at the feet of something they have made, and taking the content of their own subconscious minds as gospel! Is it not sad?

Me: I think the worst temptation of all is the temptation to abdicate responsibility, and simply 'receive,' and defer all judgments to a discarnate 'guru;' be he a genuine human soul or an etheric construction. You taught me some sharp lessons about that, my Brother, when first we began to consciously converse.

Angel: Yes. And slow you were to learn them! The Gifts of the Spirit are given to make you more human, more responsible; and they are given you for the sake of others, that all men may learn to stand on their own feet and look Life full in the face. They are perverted if they did less than that. I will be your Brother in Christ and your Guardian Angel. Call me 'Guru,' and I shall chasten you for Love's sake.

Me: If mediumship is a human to human phenomenon, by what means do I become conscious of your words to me; or Pan's for that matter?

Angel: By two different dimensions of the same basic gift. Some have one, some have another. Most of the gifted in this way are mediums, but this categorization is unsatisfactory as you know.

The gifts are given as required. That is all! Believe me, you earn no 'extra marks' for having them!

Me: We began with the evolution of consciousness. What a turn this conversation has taken! We have quite failed to stick to the point. Our hearers will wonder what it has all been about.

Angel: And that is exactly the point. Let them wonder. Come Brethren, ask yourselves what we have been saying, and how it fits together.

The Sword in the Sun

ii

Angel: Tell me of the evolution of Almighty God. Some of you mortal men talk learnedly of this.

Me: But would you understand it if I told you? The very idea seems ridiculous to me. I suspect that the 'evolution of God' idea is a way of saying that there is a progression in the Divine thoughts. God's is, after all, a *living* Mind.

Angel: Your suspicions are justified. All Creation lives, and living things are alive, and have their lives to lead within the Mind of God. There is more free will than you suppose.

Me: But the evolution of consciousness... does the consciousness, the awareness of everything, evolve? What about yourself, my Guardian Angel?

Angel: Why not? My life with you is full of surprises! Our evolution is in the depths of our experience of loving. It is a matter, you might say, of realizing potential. But the potential is infinite in its extent.

Me: And Pan? Does his consciousness evolve the same way? Is it a matter of realizing the infinite potential of his Panhood?

Angel: Yes, of course. And so it is with all his children.

Me: But the plant Devas? There has been an evolution in the very form of plants. And there was a time when there were no plants. What of this?

Angel: What of it indeed? Did not Pan tell you that they change and change and are changeless? And when were there no plants? Do not tie the whole of being to your own restricted wavelength.

Me: My cat has just interrupted us. What of her cathood? There was when cats were not!

Angel: There was not! But you shall learn of that hereafter. She could tell you many things, but now is not the time to ask her.

Me: But what of my animals? What of Fred, my dog who died?

Angel: Fred the dog? Or Fred the bird before the dog? Or Fred the fish before the bird before the dog? Or would you ask of Fred the sheep, before the fish, before the bird, before the dog? Ask of his 'Fredhood,' not of his doghood!

Me: I find this very disturbing indeed! But I suppose I would prefer a tidy universe. I would know of that Fredhood now, for I loved it more than I ever knew it possible to love an animal.

Angel: That Fredhood is beside you! In your ministry, and that of your family and friends, it is fulfilled. Oh, the wagging of tails at the Day of Judgment! Do not build your pictures or your theories upon this. This is not a sentimental doggy paradise I describe to you. It is a deeper thing by far than this, and infinitely more beautiful. A very great mystery is here.

Me: I think I dare not ask for fear I build my sentimental doggy paradises round the answers given. Or perhaps I shall not understand the answers. But this is faint hearted of me, Brother. Explain please.

Angel: Wait and see how gracious the Lord is.

Me: The evolution of consciousness — that great process which I described to you — it has some other dimension to it then? There is an identification of an *already existing consciousness* with the complexities of structures as they evolve? And what of the difference in consciousness between a sheep, a fish, a bird and a dog? Is there a fluctuation back and forth?

Angel: You are very near the truth, as near as you need get. And of these differences in consciousness which you describe, are they not differences in *experience*? Do they not resemble different dimensions of a common consciousness? I will not tell you more just now, for you are perplexed enough and your emotions are aroused at the thought of Fred.

The Sword in the Sun

iii

Me: Animal, fish, bird, animal! You have put my mind in a turmoil! Is there, here, an identification of a consciousness with the Elements? Earth, water, air and earth again? And if so, what of Fire?

Angel: You have guessed it. And your love is the Fire.

Me: And does this pattern repeat itself on earth at many levels? In the insects and their watery equivalents, and the lower animals? And then, in man, in his identification with an Element in the date of his birth into the world? Are our various incarnate lives according to a cycle?

Angel: Yes, you have it. But the cycle of incarnate lives is now fulfilled. Since the Incarnation, you have chosen that which was appropriate to your mission.

Me: The Zodiac, and its animal signs; and the Chinese twelve-year cycle of animals, are these real?

Angel: No. But they are rough and ready correspondences with a reality which they seek to interpret. Treat them with caution, for etheric thought-forms abound. It is not easy to penetrate the nonsense in order to arrive at the reality behind it. Do not dismiss them out of hand, and do not depend upon them either.

Me: But the Elements — earth, air, fire and water — are they real?

Angel: They represent realities. That is the better way of putting it.

Me: The shapes we call Platonic Solids; they are representations of the same realities. And the fifth of the solids represents the Universe itself.

Angel: Is that statement or question? Having said that, what have you said? Beware of knowledge, it will not make you a better man.

Me: I know it will not, and I know that it is easy to imagine that 'knowing things' makes one important — even 'wise!' I hope that all my understanding will make me more compassionate with myself, with other men and with the world at large. If not, it will have been a waste of time.

Angel: It is time we gave our hearers a rest. They will regard their goldfish with suspicion and wait to see a pretty girl appear! Men make fairy stories, not the fairies. Yet every fairy story has reality behind it. And look! Beware! Your cat is watching you!

iv

Angel: Let us return to the subject of prayer. Sing to me, little
Brother!

Me: What shall I sing? Is it a poem you want from me? Something
that tries to express what cannot be said in any other way? And
if so, which one?

Angel: Your Lover called you. Tell me about it.

Me: My lover called me from the bed of dawn.
And, ankle wet in the heavy grass,
I ran through a curling mist,
Ran to the old stone walls of an ancient cell;
And there, in silence heavy with love
As the waking light touched the seraph's wings,
I gave myself to my love.

My love set me down
And was gone on the wings of morning.
I wandered through the early fields
As time returned from a distant tower,
And I looked anew through his dear eyes
And saw his face in every flower.

Angel: You fear what I might ask? I respect your intimacies.

The Sword in the Sun

Me: It was an utterly transfiguring experience. I was caught up
high into the air (or so it seemed) and was ravished by Love. I
ran from the Church in case I should be seen; my own reflection in a mirror shocked me.

Angel: It was not given for your own pleasure. I was there and
rejoiced to see, it. There had been crosses to bear. You remembered one some years later. Tell me about it.

Me: I cried aloud; a wild and bitter cry.
    Bats fluttered from the eaves, a window lit,
    A murmuring of voices stirred and stilled.
    I lay in horror, staring, staring at the sky.

    Full seven years past I passed that way;
    The house has gone now, in its place
    A by-pass thunders. There remains nor trace
    Nor shade, nor memory today.

    So time and place and people move apart
    And fashions change, and seasons turn,
    And time and times run on. Beneath it all
    Eternity lies constant. All who rise (or fall)
    And face that searing darkness, burn.
    I bear the scar forever on my heart.

Angel: It was yourself you were fighting, and you thought it was
the devil! You bear the scars yet, but they are healed.

Me: Self or the devil, it is hard to tell one from another sometimes.

Angel: Too long you were identified.

Me: What do you mean? Before this present life? Before the
Incarnation?

Angel: Both; but no matter now. That battle has been won for you.
    Sing to me again.

Me: He came, as he said, a thief in the night;
    As a darkness darker than the darkness;
    Unheard, unexpected, unprepared for.

    Time tarried but a breath, a parting of the lips,
    An opening of the eyes wide; closing, infolding
    On that which pierced their lids and possessed.
    Time tarried but a stirring of the hand,
    A laying wide, a closing and infolding
    On that which pierced the naked soul
    And possessed.

               O Darkness, Darkness;
                    Holy and Mighty.

    He came, a darkness; clad in the smoke
    Of holy fire. He came as the North and
    As the South Wind, breathed upon
    His moonlit garden, and the spices flowed;
    The precious fruits were tasted, and found rest.

               O Darkness, Darkness;
                    Holy and Mighty.

    The daughters of Jerusalem, the roes and hinds
    Of the scented fields, stirred not up
    Nor wakened;
    But Time from his tall tower called:
    Time, time, time;
    It is not time,
    Submit to time,
    Be a wall of time,
    A door of time;
    There is yet time.

The Sword in the Sun

> O Darkness, Darkness;
>   Holy and Mighty,
>   Holy, Immortal:
>   Return.

Angel: What was this of which you were singing? Do you know?

Me: I hardly know. It was a terrible embrace; a ravishing. I know no other word for it. And I was sad indeed when it was past. Interpret it for me, my Brother, if you will.

Angel: A ravishing it was indeed! But that word has an unhappy meaning for mortal men, and this was Joy eternal. Others have sung of the same love-making.

Me: Yes, others whose names I dare not utter in the same breath as my own for mortal terror of presumption.

Angel: You will hang on to hierarchies, Your Lord loves the lowest dog-thief as dearly as he loves you. And does he love 'heroic saints' the more? This does not make you perfect, little Brother. Your consciousness has undergone some evolution in the dimension of prayer; it is a moral evolution, but it does not leave you faultless as your wife and children will be quick to tell you. And should you like me to remind you of a failing or two for fear you should imagine yourself a 'Saint'?

Me: I don't think I believe in 'Saints' as once I did. I think it safe for you to forego the sorrow of such dolorous reminders. I am not likely to forget my failings; they will not let me!

Angel: Men do not wind themselves aloft in prayer. You have written yourself that prayer is a matter of the will. So it is. And those who think only of 'raising consciousness' are sailing close to magic. Nevertheless, in prayer, consciousness may indeed be raised, and in prayer this is no longer magic — it is mysticism. The two could not be further apart.

Me: The classical divisions of the life of prayer represent a process of evolution, although this is not always how they are understood. I refer to the *Way of Purgation*, the *Way of Illumination* and the *Unitive Way*. These are stages in the evolution of consciousness in prayer — and in that life which is (or ought to be) 'prayer without ceasing' — but it is a moral evolution. One becomes almost a different person; the same, but morally different. This is badly put and I apologize.

Angel: Not so badly. But I would that your textbooks on the 'spiritual life' made happier reading. If I were capable of depression, they would surely make me depressed. They are full of Lent, with precious little Easter in them.

Me: I fear the realization of our Easter involves a forest of little crosses. But it is true. We make the spiritual life sound altogether too much like Sorrow. We obscure the Joy which takes all sorrow in its stride.

Angel: Sing me another little song. You were sitting, alone, on a fallen tree in the Forest of Dean. And you became aware of the Love in things. Sing to me of 'Eternity.'

Me: I sat upon a fallen tree,
And looked and saw Eternity.
The lovers thronged upon the road
And passed and passed; are passing still,
Their feet a whisper in the grass;
Their voice a wind upon the hill.

And as I sat and lingered there,
They met, and filled the shining air
'Till suddenly-all things were new!
And tree and leaf, and earth and stone,
And running water woke, and sang.
All sang for joy-save me alone.

The Sword in the Sun

I rose up from that fallen tree
And took my quest — Eternity!
I'll search the caverns of the moon
And climb the high hills of the sun
Till love and lovers fill the sky;
And they, the elements and I are one.

Angel: And with this we shall conclude our day's work. All you
who overhear: this is the way things are. Look about you!

V

Me: Now I will begin. Concerning the evolution of consciousness, Brother, has the process of reincarnation about it a measure of evolution?

Angel: Little Brother, reincarnation is the process of evolution. And upon more levels than one. What have you in mind?

Me: Many things. First, the evolution of human consciousness upon this wavelength. This has been a realization of potential upon two levels. First upon the animal level as Paleolithic man evolved; and second upon the 'truly human' level as the higher consciousness began to realize its potential by identification with an evolving creature on a lower wavelength. Am I very wrong?

Angel: A little, but not very. Don't forget, you were *destroyed*. You lost your being but retained your conscious potential, and something of your memory.

Me: And since the Incarnation? As the world progresses, man returns to a higher consciousness? The 'wheel of life' has become a spiral, upwards?

Angel: To some extent, but do not build too much on this. This age is passing and will soon be past.

Me: I think we are too quick to build theories on intuitive perceptions. Our metaphysics and our morals depend upon a mystical awareness of which they seek to be expressions. But do we not try to organize reality too much on our own terms?

Angel: Yes you do. And what big words you use to do it!

Me: And now the animals. Is there a movement between man and beast in reincarnation? Was I a horse or a dog? Might I become, perhaps, a cow?

Angel: No. The orders are quite separate. But in your animal nature on this wavelength you evolved from this lower order of being, and so man and beast are mutually identified, and shall ever be identified.

Me: But I read in an account of a long-term conscious friendship — like our own but the guardian was human — that there is the possibility of an animal becoming human. Was this guardian mistaken?

Angel: Possibly. Human guardians only know what they know, and there is much subtlety in the relationship between man and beast. Perhaps he was misunderstood. Does it matter in the least?

Me: Not at all as far as I am concerned. I am well-pleased that the essential being whom I knew as my dog Fred is fulfilled, and awaits, like me, a reunion.

Angel: Would you have him man? Or would you have him as himself? Is he not lovable because he is other than you? If he were ever to be man your relationship would be destroyed, and this would destroy a part of you, for every relationship is eternal.

Me: A terrifying thought! What of all the failed relationships, the hatreds, the bad faith and broken promises? And what of the casual way that men and women use each other? All this eternal?

Angel: The relationship is eternal, not the failure. You are attending, in this life, to failures in earlier lives, little Brother. And this is not the only way. All shall be mended, but repairs are costly.

Me: And all these debts are debts of Love, and Love determines how they shall be paid?

Angel: Love Himself has paid them all Himself. But your love may well move you to pay yourself that which has been paid by Him and thus identify yourself even more closely with both Him and your own Creditor. If Love determines this, is this a scandal to you? You have not found it so. Behold! You are here now!

Me: Yes, here without a memory. I fancy dragging up memories of former lives in this life is a thoroughly unprofitable thing to do.

Angel: Unless your name be Narcissus. And he was a silly fellow. Now come, little Brother, enough! Our hearers will grow weary of us.

The Sword in the Sun

vi

Angel: Everything is an illusion! Comment, little Brother.

Me: I once tried to write a complicated book on mysticism. It wasn't very good, but I attempted to come to terms with the Hindu idea of 'Maya' — usually translated as 'illusion.'

Angel: I know it well. It was complicated indeed. Refresh your memory from it and tell me simply: What is 'Maya?'

Me: The usual English rendering of Maya is illusion, a mirage, something that isn't there in reality. This rendering makes us imagine that those to whom the word is a basic, spiritual 'technical term' must have a despairing and cynical view of things.

Angel: Go on.

Me: As I understand it, Maya is not a state of affairs so much as a relationship. I see it as a word for describing the relationship between this phenomenal world, the world of the senses, and what Teilhard calls 'the within of things.'

Angel: Give an illustration.

Me: This vast Victorian Gothic rectory of mine, set four-square amid lawns and towering Wellingtonias. It needs a real effort of mind and will to formally acknowledge the indisputable fact that it is but an unimaginable complex of electrical charges, and that its 'mass' is but an expression of energy. And even more difficult is the realization that the hand that holds the pen is nothing different; and neither is the face which I beheld in the shaving-mirror this morning.

Angel: And upon every level of existence, every plane of being, the same is true! You saw me as a copper-coloured flame. Others see me differently, but what you see conforms to the self-same pattern. Everything is Maya: you are Maya, I am Maya. Only God Himself is otherwise. We are expressions of his thoughts and are made, if you like, of 'mind-stuff.' Call it energy if you must, I prefer to call it Love.

Me: Now we are launched upon a discussion of strange words, or so it seems. Tell me, what is Karma?

Angel: No. You tell me!

Me: Karma, as I am given to understand it, is a kind of 'balance sheet' of the human soul, kept in the heavenly records office. According to the way in which a man plays the cards given him in this incarnate life, so he will receive a better hand, or a worse one, to play in the next life. I find the idea of an inexorable cosmic computer distasteful, and as a Christian, I think I must reject it.

Angel: Must you now? Well, you are right. There are no computers in Heaven, and our Lord has wiped your slate forever clean. Yet love moves you to identify with that which has been done for you, but always freely, always of devotion. There is no reparation to Almighty God. Karma is a voluntary thing, you might say, but nothing is forgotten in Heaven. All is forgiven, nothing forgotten!

Me: Thank God for that. Now I will speak to you of 'Atman,' and since you will have me think for myself, I will say that the following terms may be mutually identified: Atman, soul, psyche, and what physicists call 'the organizing field.' All these terms represent the archetypal idea of a man as he is in the Mind of God. They are the fundamental 'set of proportions,' as a friend of mine put it, unique to every being.

Angel: Splendid! But beware of 'soul,' the word is used very loosely. 'Spirit' is better in this case as I shall explain later.

Me: Now I shall go astray. 'Brahman' is the 'world-soul' in Hindu terminology, the totality of things. The Hindu seeks to identify his Atman forever with the Brahman. There is, classically I believe, no idea of the retention of separate identity, and God is identified with his Creation altogether. Am I wrong?

Angel: Yes and no, like any two Hindus! Do not generalize, little Brother. The Hindu Scriptures record a multitude of insights, some so orthodox to you as to satisfy your most particular theologian. Others less so. The interpretation is left to private judgment. Read them in the Light of Christ, and see him everywhere.

Me: Another way of speaking of Atman and Brahman is to say that man is the Microcosm and God is the Macrocosm. This seems to me to be unsatisfactory. Man is made in God's image in that he reflects the nature of the eternal Mind, reflective and creative, loving and personal. But this terminology that I have mentioned seems to suggest that either man is God writ small, or God is man writ large. It will not do.

Angel: No, it will not do. These are Western European terms and they attempt to define and restrict within a definition. Atman and Brahman are Asian terms, and Asians have more sense than to seek to define the indefinable. That is why the Hindu words are so satisfactory — man can never quite discover their meaning!

Me: Very well then; Yin and Yang, the two polarities. What of them?

Angel: What indeed? You have said it all! Yang is the archetypal masculine principle, Yin the archetypal feminine. At least, these are the words you use if you are Chinese.

Me: I catch myself out. I am being 'wise' again. The learned recitation of esoteric words makes a man think that he is attaining to some Ancient Wisdom.

Angel: Am I, an angel, to make myself wise by the solemn trading in words like 'nuts and bolts.' I should shake Heaven with the laughter I should provoke. O Man! Will you never see how ridiculous you are? If you love our Lord and know yourself loved what need have you of 'wisdom?'

Me: On that note, Brother, let us end. I can no longer take my wisdom seriously.

vii

Angel: Let us return to the subject of prayer. What is prayer?

Me: Prayer is a dialogue of wills, not words. I suppose you could call it 'giving our Lord your undivided attention.' And yet there are two dimensions of it: there are indeed these times of undivided attention, but there is also the unceasing *personal relationship*. Both are prayer.

Angel: Well done! As you have written somewhere else, prayer and marriage have much in common. The relationship *is*, and life is lived *within* the relationship. But the vitality of the relationship depends upon the times of undivided attention, either to other. There is a total, mutual giving of self, on several different levels. And no two persons are quite alike.

Me: The mystics call our Lord the 'Heavenly Bridegroom,' and I know what they mean. The mystical encounter with him in prayer is intensely 'Bridal.' It has a nuptial quality, and the femininity of the human soul is quite a shock to discover. Am I talking nonsense? I don't think so.

Angel: You know you are not. Why are you so shy of talking of prayer? The Church is called the Bride of Christ, and she is able to be called the Body of Christ because, in human marriage, Bride and Bridegroom are 'one flesh.' It is very simple.

Me: And the Eucharist is the Marriage Supper.

Angel: The Eucharist is many things, but it is indeed the Marriage Supper, and the Bridal Bed as well. The human instinct which speaks of 'bed and board' in the same breath is true indeed.

Me: We are shy of using nuptial terms. We have a quite unbalanced reticence about them.

Angel: What would the Fall derange if it were not the place of greatest beauty? The devil is the father of obscenity, but we shall not speak of him now.

Me: May we return to the idea of the evolution of consciousness in prayer. I fancy 'evolution' is a misleading word. Is 'growth' a better one?

Angel: Evolution, growth, development — take your pick. Now tell me what I have already told you, but at another time.

Me: There are seven 'degrees' of prayer, corresponding to seven levels of consciousness. They are as follows:

1. Posture and gesture.
2. The Dance.
3. Music and song.
4. Vocal prayer, both private and corporate.
5. Prayerful meditation, affective prayer, the prayer of quiet and infused contemplation.
6. The prayer of union, called in the East, 'Samadhi.'
7. The prayer of ecstatic union, rapture, and the spiritual marriage (which last is an abiding state rather than an 'experience' of prayer).

Angel: Splendid! There are many terminologies. Some talk of 'the seventh heaven' and St. Paul, 'the third heaven;' both to prayer in that final, seventh degree.

Me: The excitements of prayer wear off. The explosion of the emotions does not keep recurring in the mystical degrees.

Angel: Would you have it recur? Is it not exhausting, and irrelevant?

Me: My cat has interrupted us again, What is the degree of her prayer? I cannot think that she does not pray.

Angel: She is prayer. She is posture, gesture and the Dance. There is more, far more to it than this, but it would be unprofitable to attempt an explanation.

Me: And what of ghastly boredom and aridity? What of the Dark Nights of the Soul, dear Brother? I think them morally necessary, and I know them profitable, but they are misery to undergo.

Angel: They serve to train your fallen will. Endure them, thankfully if you can. You endure as much or as little as you need and always you look back on them with gratitude.

Me: Are we to seek for mystical experience? I know the answer, but I would hear it again.

Angel: Do you know the answer? Seek our Lord Himself and none other, and everything that is profitable shall attend your search. And the Lord alone is the judge of what is profitable.

The Sword in the Sun

viii

Angel: Now let us return to the evolution of consciousness; how do you understand this now, little Brother?

Me: There is a great deal more to it than I would have supposed. We can only catch a glimpse of one dimension after another, all different, and on many different planes, and about many different things. All seem to mutually interact, but it is hard for us to know where to begin in an attempt to comprehend it all.

Angel: You cannot begin to comprehend it all. What you see is a multitude of tiny facets of the life of a living organism of which you are a tiny part. As soon as you exalt one facet and make one of your 'isms' out of it, you lose the vision of the rest of them.

Me: I remember a mental image I found within my head, a kind of vision I suppose. It was of a sphere with lines of latitude and longitude running, this way and that, all over it. I realized that these were time-scales, and that time was endless but finite, and that all these time-scales, and indeed every moment upon every scale, met in the *NOW* which was the center of the sphere. It was a rough and ready image, but it serves to illustrate the evolution of the thoughts of an Eternal Mind, This is what we are dealing with, is it not?

Angel: Well done. Look at the *process* going on in things, and see how God is thinking, But remember, you are but a tiny thought in this same Mind. Do not make an 'ism' of your vision.

Me: I remember how this mental image changed until it was the Host, as I hold it in my hands at the Consecration of the Eucharist. The sum of things, and the whole of the vitality of things — 'this is my Body!' And yet this was not Pantheism.

Angel: You and your 'isms!' Is not Pantheism the destruction of a vision by the foolish attempt to define its mystery? Go on.

Me: And then I became aware of the fact that the sphere was indeed a sphere. Not a disc-like picture of a sphere in a book. I was suddenly terrified by the thought of *volume*! The sheer volume of eternity was too much for me to contemplate.

Angel: And how much more the reality, full of dimensions of which you have no possibility of knowing? But courage, little Brother! Perfect Love casts out fear. And now we leave our hearers to meditate upon these things. Hearken to what speaks to you; leave the rest.

The Tree of Life

i

Angel: Now let us talk about the Tree of Life. Tell me about your spine, little Brother.

Me: Never would I have associated the two ideas. But since you ask me, I will tell you what you yourself have told me about the 'chakras.'

Angel: I have not told you much. I have confirmed what others have told you. Tell me of the chakras.

Me: They are seven in number, and aligned as it were down the spinal column, but not identified with it. They begin at the crown of the head — the crown chakra. Then comes the 'ajna' chakra between the eyes and a little above them. Then come the throat chakra, the heart chakra, the solar plexus, the sacral regions and, finally, the soles of the feet. These are focal points of energy and relate to various levels of consciousness. I note that others speak of another chakra at the spleen.

Angel: Yes, there is another at the spleen, and indeed there are many more, but they are secondary. You say the chakras are not identified with the spinal column. Neither are they, but the spinal column is identified with them. Go on.

Me: Many things are related to the chakras. There are, classically, three 'parts' of man: body, soul and spirit. These are unsatisfactory terms unless they are elaborated. It is better to speak of Lower Man, Rational Man and Spiritual Man. This is the three-fold nature as it was known, I believe, to the 'kahunas' of Hawaii — the medicine men, priests, or whatever they were. And to other primitive people as well.

Angel: And all these terms are capable of misunderstanding; none are satisfactory. Sit lightly to them all and avoid constructing 'isms.' Go on.

Me: The top two chakras, the crown and the ajna, relate to Spiritual Man. The throat chakra relates to Rational Man, and the rest relate to Lower Man. But to say this is to run the risk of wild misunderstanding. One does not, for example, cut a man's head off at the throat and send that bit to Heaven!

Angel: The Post Office might not accept it! Go on.

Me: You drive me hard! The chakras relate to seven levels of consciousness — the degrees of prayer relate to the same — and it is convenient, but potentially misleading, to talk of seven 'bodies.' There are seven planes or expressions of the being of man, all interrelated. I grow nervous. I fear I shall be unclear and sound more eccentric than I am.

Angel: It depends who is the eccentric, you or the one who overhears you. No matter. Go on.

Me: Very well then; from the bottom up. The chakra at the feet *relates to* the physical body in this world — 'cut it and it bleeds' — that body. The sacral chakra relates to the etheric body, the matrix of the physical, that which holds the physical body together. It is the final transference of consciousness to the etheric body at death, and the severing of the connection with the physical, which causes the physical body to decay. Some sensitive people talk of a 'silver cord' — a kind of umbilical chord — between them.

Angel: Never mind the 'silver cord.' This relates to an abnormal state, and a dangerous one at that. Go on.

Me: The solar plexus chakra relates to the electromagnetic body, or rather 'field.' It is an energy-field, sometimes known as the 'aura.' Some sensitives can see the aura clairvoyantly, and its general health and state are reflected in color. Am I right?

Angel: Yes; go on.

Me: The heart chakra relates to the Astral or Emotional body. This is the inner core of the lower man, the vehicle of incarnation. All these we have in common with the animals? The higher mammals at least?

Angel: Yes, the higher mammals certainly, but let us confine our attentions to man. This is not a course of instruction for esoteric vets. I am glad you stressed the fact that the various chakras *relate to* the various levels of consciousness, or 'bodies.' It is great nonsense to identify them.

Me: The throat chakra relates to rational man; 'soul' as opposed to 'spirit' — but these words are unsatisfactory. Rational man is the 'fallen' part. Poor lower man bears great burdens of guilt which are not his to bear. Rational man is incarnate in the lower man. But the Fall cut him off from his fullness which is spiritual man, the Atman, the archetype forever in Heaven.

Angel: Guilt is irrelevant to lower man, but he bears great burdens of it which do him mischief at every level. It is rational man who is deranged; separated, as you said, from his Higher Self, his 'super-ego'— if you like that term — but restored to it in principle by our Lord. The fulfillment of that principle depends upon the living out of that relationship begun in Baptism.

Me: But it is possible for man in this life, Baptized or not, and even before the Incarnation, to have some contact with the higher self. The ajna chakra, relating to what might be called the 'aspirational self or body' is a kind of wireless aerial for this.

Angel: Yes, some contact certainly, or man would be utterly destroyed. But I refer to *total union*. It is this fully integrated man whose is the Body of the Resurrection. The Resurrection Body is the expression, by the principle of Maya which we have discussed, of the Higher Self itself — the spiritual man, the spirit, Atman, call it what you will. And as I have told you, it has a multitude of 'lower man' suits in its eternal wardrobe. This Resurrection Body comes and goes at will, and transcends every plane of being. Our Lord, in his Resurrection and Ascension, demonstrated this. He showed how man shall be. What else do you think he was doing?

Me: It will not do to isolate parts of human experience and lock them up in watertight compartments. Life is a unity. The chakras are relevant to health and healing at every level, to prayer at every level, and indeed to the whole being of man. One begins to see the absurdity of isolating Sunday from the rest of the week!

Angel: But do you really see it? The very days are chakras of the human time-scale, Why do you think a week has seven days? Now tell me about it. Think!

Me: I had never thought of this before. From the bottom up, then:

> *Monday*: a coming down to earth with a bump! The feet.
>
> *Tuesday*: a neither-one-thing-nor-the-other day. Etheric. The sacrum.
>
> *Wednesday*: The solar plexus. The pit of the week's stomach.
>
> *Thursday*: The heart. A lightening, a prefiguring. Maundy Thursday. Ascension Day. Corpus Christi.
>
> *Friday:* Rational man, fallen and deranged. Good Friday.
>
> *Saturday*: Aspiration. The Jewish Sabbath. Weekend, relaxation.
>
> *Sunday*: The crown chakra. The Resurrection. The Eucharist. Heaven.

Angel: Precisely. And now we will let our hearers brood upon the unfamiliar thoughts presented to them. Do not worry, Brethren, if you cannot take to this. Let it pass. We do not seek to convert.

ii

Angel: Now we shall return to the subject of prayer. Sing to me again, little Brother.

Me: Yes, but what? I cannot think of anything appropriate to our present discussion.

Angel: As we have not yet begun the discussion, that is not surprising. Sing to me of Oakenhill Wood. The trees were not oaks; they were conifers, but no matter.

Me: Now is a slow, unfolding moment
    Perpetually present. Here is always now.
    Time passed with the track's end,
    And my stride shortened, and slowed, and stilled,
    And stopped, soft-carpeted in deep silence.

    Here is a universe of tall trees;
    Trunk after trunk to the world's end,
    Numberless, endless, silent.
    And here my consciousness, here my priesthood
    Sees, and loves, and animates.

    Here the Word looks through created eyes
    Adoring in creation the Creator. Here
    Is Love; and now, the Trinity.

Angel: 'The Word looks through created eyes adoring in creation the Creator.' That was well said. That is your priesthood, little Brother; it is the priesthood of man.

Me: Why does a poet write of what he does not know when he writes it? I understand that poem, and others, so much better now than when I wrote it.

Angel: So does Isaiah! Poetry expresses truths on many different levels. Very seldom does the poet understand more than one or two of the levels when he is writing. And that is why academic criticism of poetry is usually false to the very nature of poetry. Any poet will tell you that the textbooks talk the most sublime nonsense about his poems. They were not written like that at all. Poetry and the Scriptures — all Scriptures — have much in common. But not all poetry is Scripture.

Me: Our Lord, in his Incarnate Life, taught poetically. And some scholars believe he taught, very often at least, in poetry.

Angel: You are right, but never talk of 'merely poetry.' Poetry is always more, never less. And now, sing to me again; and of the same wood. 'Paths of Glory' is your title.

Me: It is, I think, the sudden stillness,
   The stillness of a tall, a slender tree,
   The narrow, arrow-straightness of the path,
   The unexpected consciousness of 'now,'
   That grips, evokes and beckons;
   Lifts high the latch of mystery.

   You cannot tread that way. Your feet
   Will kick the door shut as they run.
   This path is not for treading; it does not lead,
   Like that, to anywhere, like that.
   Rather, it is its destination;
   Full-known and fully-trod when first begun.

Angel: 'This path is not for treading.' Why? Because 'it is its destination.' Our Lord is 'the Way' and you were speaking of Him. Did you know that?

Me: No! At least, not consciously. But it was the *Life*, the vibrancy, the sense of expectation, the sense of 'at any moment!' and 'now!' all mixed up together, that gripped me. I owe much to those woods.

Angel: And they to you for being their priest. You had much to do with Pan, did you not?

Me: Yes indeed! But I neither knew of Pan nor took the idea of his Children seriously. And yet, I think I *almost* knew them consciously. You shall have another poem:

> A moment sooner and I might have seen them
> Dancing on the mossy floor, or sitting out
> Under the shade of fungi on tree roots;
> But I came crashing through the snapping twigs
> And drove them far in sudden fright
> Through that open door of sunlight
> Slanting through the dark trunks, deep
> In green, mysterious silence.
>
> I have seen
> Their shadows vanish once before,
> Under a limestone cliff; leaving
> behind a sharp dank incense smell,
> Brown, green and earthy, as I
> Crunched heavy on the jungle path.
>
> I will build a little forest shrine;
> And they, the squirrel, and the snuffling rat,
> And I, shall worship there.

Angel: And did you build that shrine?

Me: Yes, in my heart. I know no other place.

Angel: There is no other place. Did I not say that we should be speaking of prayer, little Brother?

The Sword in the Sun

iii

Angel: Let us talk about the chakras. Tell me of the ajna chakra.

Me: This is called the 'third eye' by some people, but it is the chakra through which both spiritual and psychical phenomena are perceived by those gifted with the appropriate sensitivities.

Angel: Distinguish between spiritual and psychical.

Me: The spiritual overlaps the psychical, but the psychical does not overlap the spiritual. The same psychic 'muscles' are used in each case. But to distinguish between them: I would say that the spiritual has to do with Heaven and is always within the context of prayer, whereas the psychical usually has to do with the inner dimension of earth. Very roughly, the psychical includes the contents of the unconscious mind, both individual and collective, and the etheric dimension — a very earth-bound thing. But this is hard to define, and to a non-psychic, I shall seem to be talking so much nonsense.

Angel: The spiritual always has to do with prayer. You will remember an occasion in your ministry — indeed more than one occasion — when you became aware of four distinct phenomena. You became aware to the point of clairvoyant vision on one occasion of the Holy Angels. Similarly, you became aware of human souls present, but in a heavenly dimension. On one occasion at least you had clairvoyant vision of them. These you perceived, in every manner of your perception, through your ajna chakra.

You also perceived more than one soul earthbound in his etheric body. And to those you ministered as a priest in a very ordinary priestly way. You also — but let us not dwell on this —

perceived a demon, and again with clairvoyant vision upon one occasion. These two you also perceived through your ajna chakra. The first two were in the spiritual dimension, the last two in the purely psychical dimension. You will remember that you were deeply in prayer and prayerful recollection for the last two. Indeed, had you not been recollected for your encounter with the fourth that I mentioned, you would most certainly have died.

Me: Theology distinguished between Grace and Nature, and Grace is the perfection and fulfillment of Nature, and transcends it. In a nutshell, therefore, may we not say that the psychical is of Nature, and the Spiritual is of Grace which fulfills, perfects and transcends the psychical? In prayer there is no magic, it is transformed into mysticism. Nature and Grace again.

Angel: Well done! Now what about the crown chakra?

Me: I am guessing. But an objective, personal encounter with the Lord himself, such as St. Paul had on the Damascus Road, and many, many since have had ...

Angel: ... is perceived via the crown chakra. This is the chakra of prayer. *All* degrees of prayer pass through it.

Me: We have called the seven chakras the Tree of Life. Is there not another Tree, or do all 'Trees' correspond?

Angel: There are several, and they correspond. But we shall think of this anon. This will suffice for the moment.

iv

Angel: Tell me about the Qabalah. What is it?

Me: The Qabalah is of Jewish origin. It is what is known as a 'glyph,' a diagram which seeks to express inner truths pictorially as an aid to meditation upon them. The Qabalah is a diagram showing a pattern of spheres and of lines joining them. The spheres are ten in number and the lines or 'paths' are twenty-two in number. The whole represents the ten cardinal numbers and the twenty-two letters of the Hebrew alphabet — all, that is, by which rational expression may be made by man. It adds up, traditionally, to the Name of God.

Angel: How are the spheres arranged in the diagram?

Me: They are known as the Sephiroth, and they are arranged in three vertical columns. The left-hand column, or 'pillar,' is known as the Pillar of Severity, and the right-hand column is known as the Pillar of Mercy. These correspond to the archetypal feminine and masculine principles; Yin and Yang respectively.
   The middle column is called the Pillar of Equilibrium, or sometimes, the Pillar of Consciousness. There are three Sephiroth in each of the flanking pillars, and four (with the 'ghost' of a fifth) in the Pillar of Consciousness.

Angel: How do the Sephiroth relate horizontally?

Me: In three triangles. *The Supernal Triangle* connects the top three, and its apex is upwards. *The Moral Triangle* connects the next three down, and its apex is downwards. *The Psychological Triangle* is below this, with its apex downwards. And hanging as a pendant from this apex is the tenth Sephirah of all. In the Hebrew tradition this is the *Shekinah*, the archetype of Israel. In the occult tradition, this is called the 'Kingdom,' the physical world. Occultism sees the whole thing as a pattern of manifestation. It must sound very complicated.

Angel: It does! Let us have a diagram.

Me: I will give the Sephiroth their numbers; their names are unimportant for the time being:

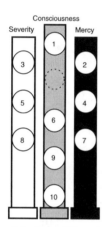

The Three Pillars

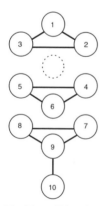

The Three Triangles

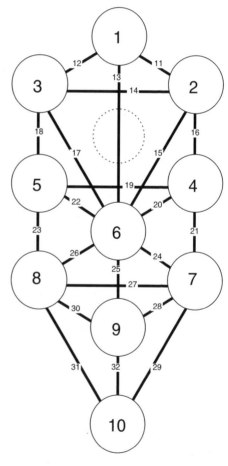

Sephiroth and Paths

Angel: Now explain the idea of manifestation to me.

Me: The first Sephirah, Kether or the Crown, represents the idea of God manifesting Himself at all. I think we may dispense with the idea of 'manifestation' and talk about 'creation' which is quite a different idea, and I believe a more truthful one. But you asked of manifestation?

Angel: I did. Go on.

Me: The second Sephirah, Wisdom, represents a *force*. This force is counterbalanced by the third Sephirah, Understanding, which is a *form*. Force is always constrained by form, in this way of thinking. These three — the *idea* of manifestation, Wisdom the force, and Understanding Wisdom constrained into form — represent the Supernal Triangle. Between this and all else is the 'abyss.' But more of that later.

Angel: Yes indeed! Much more of that later. Go on.

Me: The force overflows in manifestation upon a lower arc, as the fourth Sephirah, Mercy. This is counterbalanced by the fifth, Severity — Mercy constrained. The point of equilibrium is reached at the sixth Sephirah, Beauty, which is 'The Crown' on a lower arc. These three Sephiroth form the Moral Triangle.

Angel: And then?

Me: The force overflows again, as the seventh Sephirah, Victory. This is counterbalanced and constrained by Glory, and an equilibrium is found at The Foundation, number nine. These three form the Psychological Triangle — the former triangle, but again on a lower arc.

Angel: And the tenth Sephirah, on its own?

Me: 'The Kingdom,' in this tradition, is the phenomenal world: matter, the world of the senses. This is the completion of manifestation. But I am not happy about God 'manifesting.' To me

He is Creator, not Manifester. Notice how force is masculine and form feminine. The center contains the two in equilibrium.

Angel: And now relate the Sephiroth on the Pillar of Consciousness to the chakras of the human body!

Me: I see!

> *Kether*, 'the Crown' — the crown chakra.
>
> *Tiphareth*, 'Beauty' — the heart chakra.
>
> *Yesod*, 'the Foundation' — the sacral chakra.
>
> *Malkuth*, 'the Kingdom' — the feet.

Angel: Yes indeed. And what of the Abyss?

Me: Rational man fallen. The throat chakra. Of course!

Angel: Never mind about 'manifestation.' The insights of the Qabalah are deeper by far than the theories that are built around it. Sit lightly to it and it will come alive for you, as we shall see. Make one of your 'isms' of it and it will quickly die. Now relate man to the triangles for me.

Me: The Supernal Triangle: Spiritual Man. The Crown Sephirah is the crown chakra, and Wisdom and Understanding together form the ajna chakra. Rational Man is fallen out of the picture, I think. He is the 'Abyss!'

Angel: Yes, this is a pre-Christian concept, but we shall rediscover him before we are done.

Me: The whole of the rest is Lower Man. I cannot find the solar plexus chakra, but does it matter?

Angel: Not at all. The essential correspondence between two 'Trees of Life' is clear. We shall return to both anon.

The Tree of Life

V

Angel: It is time we spoke again to Pan. Ask him of the Tree of Life, little Brother; he is beside you now.

Me: Brother Pan. Tell me, please, of the Tree of Life.

Pan: It is the way of life, little Brother!

Me: The way of life? What do you mean?

Pan: The way by which life is lived, and life created.

Me: I have visions of a kind of structure, like the spine, or the Qabalah.

Pan: It is a tree; look at a tree.

Angel: Are you perplexed? Think of the family tree, the diagram of evolving species. It is a veritable tree — and it is also the way!

Me: Then Pan is giving me a lesson in science. That is the last thing I expected.

Angel: What is Pan if not a scientist? But I fear your learned scholars would look askance at you if you suggested that they ask the King of the Fairies when they have a knotty problem.

Pan: I construct, and my children construct; and all by the Tree; and all on the Way.

Me: 'I am the Way!' And might our Lord not also have said, 'I am the Tree?'

Angel: Read your Bible! Does it not tell you of the seraph with a flaming sword barring the way to the Tree of Life? That concerns the Fall, little Brother.

Me: So our Lord is the archetype of all things? And are all things made in the image of God, each according to its order?

Pan: What other image is there?

Me: So the Tree of Life, for Pan, is the blueprint by which all things with which he has to do are constructed in that image of God which is according to their order. And it is the Way; the principle and practice by which he lives and works. Am I right?

Pan: Correct! It is very simple. I do not understand the difficulty.

Angel: And the correspondence with the other Trees? The chakras and the Qabalah? Tell me, little Brother.

Me: The Christ Himself, Archetype and Creator of all things. He is that of which all things are images.

Angel: And now hear the orders of living beings as they were created:

> The Father, introspective, sees Himself, the Son,
> Standing upon his mental stage.
> The Son will have some fellow-players,
> And, out of Love, brings them to life.
> First, the Archangels to construct the stage
> With Angels helping.
> Then comes Man,
> Stage manager.
> The cast: a Pan
> For every world the angels make;
> And Elemental beings everywhere;
> Spirits of rock, and field, and hill,
> Devas of plants and Elements;
> And all constructed, all alive,
> Formed firm by Him who made them, of his Love.

Me: Let me relate this to the Qabalah. You have spoken of this before:

1. Kether, the Crown. The indwelling Christ.
2. Wisdom. The Archangels of Creation.
3. Understanding. The whole order of Angels.
— The Abyss. Man.
4. Mercy. Elemental Hierarchs. Pan.
5. Severity. Elemental Spirits.
6. Beauty. Devas of plant life.
7. Victory. Devas of geographical locations.
8. Glory. Devas of earth, air, fire and water.
9. Foundation.
0. The Kingdom. The expression of every form of life.
'The Kingdom,' consort of the Christ.

Angel: What of number nine?

Me: You did not mention it in your verse. But I understand it to be the whole of animal life — insects and all — on this wavelength. Why did you not mention it?

Angel: You tell me.

Me: Because Yesod, the Foundation, is the 'Abyss' (known also as 'Knowledge') fallen from its place. It was created to save man when he fell. It is the lowest order of living being.

Angel: And you are redeemed to Kether, the Crown! Did I not tell you that the Qabalah would come alive if you sat lightly to it? Do not take it more seriously than this, but it has much to tell you yet.

Pan: I return to my children. Call me, little Brother, when you will.

Angel: Our hearers: Sit lightly to what you have heard. Take what speaks to you. Leave the rest.

The Sword in the Sun

vi

Angel: You are worried, little Brother. What is the matter?

Me: I am suddenly sickened by big words and esoteric ideas. I am sick of the Qabalah, and of the chakras, and of all these complicated concepts. I only want my Lord.

Angel: Then you shall have Him! This is a blessed sickness, little Brother. Did I not tell you what a folly 'wisdom' was?

Me: And yet you led me along that same way. Why?

Angel: I have led you along many foolish ways, little Brother. And you have learned the foolishness of them thereby. You have thought for yourself and made your own decisions. This is good; this is what it is to be a man.

Me: And yet I cannot throw these concepts overboard entirely. Having sickened of them, I find that they return — but more meekly, if you understand me.

Angel: Yes I understand you. The concepts are man-made, they are your servants. They represent attempts by mortal man to understand the Universe in which he lives. There is not a thing called a Qabalah hanging in the sky. Your chakras do not flash colored lights or make a noise; your neighbors would be much perplexed if they did that! They are subjective counterparts of an objective reality. These Sanskrit words, and Hebrew words, and esoteric sounding formulae are not like knobs and levers, to be pressed and pulled in some great cosmic engine room. They are the vocabulary man has learned in order to express some things — a very few — which he has intuitively perceived and which he has been taught to help him be more human. That is all.

Me: Thank you, Brother Angel. I had grown so weary of words. But mortal man must have concepts for his mind to grasp, and the Tree of Life is a useful concept. Our Lord said of it, 'I am the Vine.'

Angel: And he went on to say, 'you are the branches. Abide in me and bear much fruit, for apart from me you can do nothing.' There is your Tree of Life, little Brother. And Pan's Tree too.

Me: I am restored! But some Qabalists try to fit our Lord into their system, and find a place for him at 'Beauty,' with Buddha, Krishna, Akhnaton, and others like them. This is quite wrong.

Angel: Yes, quite wrong. But at least their error is understandable. These 'Avatars' as they call them, or rather quaintly, 'bearers of the Christ force,' prefigured the Incarnation, but on a lower, merely human arc. They are right about them, but wrong about our Lord.

Me: So if I am to be a Qabalist, I must see our Lord as Kether, 'the Crown,' upon whom all else depends?

Angel: Yes indeed. But if you are a Qabalist, then you have made an 'ism' of the thing, and error is upon you. Sit lightly to these man-made things.

Me: May I ask of 'Avatars'? What of the Buddha, Krishna and Akhnaton? Who were they? What did they do? And whence did they come?

Angel: They were men; indeed they are men. Much fantasy has been built upon their mortal lives by other men; on Krishna in particular. You ask, 'What did they do?' They spoke of that which they had seen. What more can a man do? You ask from whence they came. From God, like every other creature. You did not ask me, 'are they blessed, and to be honored above other men?' Do you wish to know this?

Me: Yes I do.

Angel: Then rank them with the Saints of God. But I forgot, you no longer believe in 'the Saints!'

Me: Oh! Yes I do! But it seems to be necessary for a man or woman to have been dead a hundred years before it is possible for us to be objective. Don't ask me to define an 'heroic Saint.' I think I know one when I see one, but I can't define what it is I see.

Angel: The less you attempt to define, the closer you are to the Light. I would that you remembered this. Our hearers, think on this.

The Sword in the Sun

vii

Angel: Let us return again to the subject of Prayer. What is intercession, little Brother?

Me: Intercession is prayer to Almighty God on behalf of other people, or for particular causes. It is an expression of love for them and it is our Christian duty. We are to love others as fully and as much as we love ourselves.

Angel: Are you telling the Almighty what to do? Or are you giving him information which he might not have? Or do you think him either unwilling or incapable of looking after others than yourself without your prompting?

Me: You have touched upon every sense of unreality that attends our attempts at intercession. And I give you a simple answer to all your questions: No.

Angel: Then what do you think you are doing?

Me: When I intercede, I make an *act of will*, and I identify my will, — my whole being — with God's love for that person for whom I pray. I may use words. I may not. These are not important. But my willed identification with God's love for that person is my intercession. And I believe most strongly that I am privileged to be a channel through which Divine Grace can flow when I do this thing. And I believe equally strongly that it pleases God, of his mercy — and of his humility — to accept my offering and *involve me in his loving care* for others. That is what I am doing.

Angel: Indeed you are! That is intercession. You have told me of persons, what of causes?

Me: I lay them before the Lord in love. I cannot judge if they be right or not. I can only think as best I can about them, and trust my Lord to correct my faulty intentions and to use me, if he will, as a channel of Grace as before.

Angel: You can do no more, and what you do, you do well. Now tell me of Petition.

Me: Petition is prayer on one's own behalf. I think I learn to ask God to show me what my needs are. More and more I place *issues* before him, not specific things. And always, 'nevertheless not my will but thine be done.' My Lord has taught me that in Gethsemane, but it goes hard to say it sometimes. And more and more I use — and commend to others — a prayer of St. Teresa: 'Lord, show me what to do and make me do it!' A terrible prayer, but life is simpler for the praying of it. And again; more and more I know, and tell others, that 'All shall be well, and all shall be well, and all manner of thing shall be well.' After all, it doesn't matter what happens; it is what we do with what happens that matters. And more and more the tenor of petition is that I shall simply Glorify God, and he be glorified in us. I have written bravely, and I mean it. Alas, I do not always behave like that, as you know well!

Angel: It is the matter of being the branch of the Vine, and learning to *abide*, is it not?

Me: Yes. And if only we would learn just to *abide*, then we should find everything done, and done *in us and through us*, and not just *by* us.

Angel: Now tell me of Penitence and Thanksgiving.

Me: Together? In the same breath? But of course they are together and in the same breath. May I do so shortly by saying that in our learning to *abide*, we do not so much make or perform penitence and thanksgiving as *become* them. More and more I think — I hope — I *am* penitence, and more and more I *am* thanksgiving. The first gives spice and glory to the second.

Angel: You and your spice and glory! Do you not also *become* intercession? And does your Petition not turn into Adoration until you *become* Adoration?

Me: So the five parts of prayer become three. And man, the five-pointed star, becomes God, the three-in-one. I am being esoteric; I apologize.

Angel: Is Christ an esotericist? Yet this is what he has done for you. Let our hearers think on this.

The Sword in the Sun

viii

Angel: The Tree of Life; how do you understand it, little Brother?

Me: In many different ways, all fragmentary. Our Lord died upon the Tree, and He is alive. He *is* the Tree of Life, and all our understandings of the Tree must be seen in his light and in relationship to Him.

Angel: Go on.

Me: The Qabalah is an expression of his personality — the personality that creates living beings for the love of them, and for the delight of being with them. It helps us if we refrain from taking it too seriously — to see ourselves in his light, and to see the simplicity of our apparent complexity. It indicates to us something — only something — of our own 'manifestation' into this world. Our own, not His. But it is a pretty toy of a thing to make a helpful picture with, no more. Profound indeed, but no more than profound.

Angel: And the chakras?

Me: They tell us something of ourselves. They are a working hypothesis that *works*. I have experienced this working in the ministry of healing. They represent realities; and the pattern of them relates to the common archetype of 'Trees.' But it will not do to make an 'ism' of them either. Take note of them, work with them when appropriate, let them teach a fuller understanding of the nature of man, but take them no more seriously than that.

Angel: Well done! None of these things matter in the last resort. Reincarnation does not matter, nor Brahman, nor Atman, nor

Maya, nor Karma, nor Yin and Yang. All these are nuts and bolts and representations of realities. The Fall does not matter anymore. No! It does not! As the Jews forgot Adam and attended to Abraham, so do you forget Adam and attend to Christ. St. Paul will not praise you if you don't!

Me: So nothing matters save the Lord who loves us and who redeemed us, and that redemption that he won for us.

Angel: Nothing! Nothing at all. And with this clear inside your head you are a free man and may use these esoteric-sounding toys as tools to work with, to take up and put down. For one will fit one situation, one another. Then all return to the toolbox, which is Christ Himself. And he alone is the Tree of Life.

Divine Identification

i

Angel: Tell me of our Lord's Incarnation, little Brother. How do you understand it?

Me: The eternal Son of God — a poetic term which we cannot begin to understand — became incarnate. He 'took flesh,' as we say, of the Blessed Virgin Mary and was born fully man, and at the same time fully God. He united within his Incarnate Self both Godhead and manhood. As the Athanasian Creed puts it: 'not by conversion of Godhead into flesh, but by taking manhood into God.' In other words, God was not identified with man, but rather, man was identified with God. Our Lord's manhood was — indeed is — the totality of manhood in microcosm. Is that satisfactory?

Angel: Yes, as far as it goes. But what was the object of the exercise?

Me: Our Lord came to rescue man from his sinful state. We use many different words: redeem, ransom, deliver, save — but we may, I think, state the case simply by saying that our Lord came to identify the whole fallen human condition with Himself, *and to undergo it*, that it might truly be so identified. He came in order that, through identification of the human condition with Himself, the sinfulness inherent in it might be done away, and its whole circumstances turned into a means of Grace and Glory.

Angel: Very well! And your poetic words — redeem, ransom, deliver, save — they represent man's best attempts to express what has been accomplished for him. But you have almost turned these words into 'isms,' have you not?

Me: Yes. And when we do that, our depth and breadth of vision suffers. St. Anselm expressed the redemption in terms of Medieval knightly honor. It helped man's understanding at the time, but then that idea died and Anselm's way of expressing things began to constrict rather than to expand man's understanding. I hope I am not being unfair to St. Anselm?

Angel: No, not so long as you recognize that future generations may say as much about you! You have said everything that matters; it is the identification of the whole, fallen human condition with the Lord Himself that is important. The implications for man are infinite.

Me: One of the early Fathers of the Church said; 'God became man in order that man might become God.' We fell from our place into the lowest place, and we are redeemed out of it into the highest. We dance, hereafter, at the center of the ring, with the Lord of the Dance Himself.

Angel: Yes; that is your potential. Not all will realize that potential.

Me: And what of those that do not? This realization is the action of Grace perfecting Nature; it requires total identification of wills, human and Divine. But what of the recalcitrant? Are there degrees of salvation, or of realization?

Angel: No; it is all or nothing. With our Lord it is always all or nothing. There are no fences to sit on.

Me: And what of those for whom it is 'nothing?'

Angel: For them it is nothing; that is all. Their wills are free; the choice is their own.

Me: This 'nothing,' is it destruction? Or is it a kind of fallen 'status quo?' Is it my business to ask this question now?

Angel: No. Not now; but later on we shall return to it. All you who overhear; turn to your Bibles. Hear the words of our Lord.

The Sword in the Sun

ii

Angel: Sing to me of the Divine Identification, little Brother.

Me: What shall I sing? I can think of nothing I have written that
   speaks of this.

Angel: Nothing? Sing to me of 'May Hill.'

Me: There is a sacramental something here;
      A sighing in the tall trees,
      And the grass, alive and whispering;
      Speaking to an elemental faculty.

      I have known this elemental thing before;
      It has caught me helpless, unawares,
      Splashing naked in a mountain stream
      or scrambling up through heather on high hills;

      It has stunned me with a raging, wild desire:
      'To be one with this place!
      'With this hill to be one! — '
      And left me limp and staring. My sudden spasm
      Stilled, I've turned and climbed more slowly on.

      But here is quietness; the dreadful chasm bridged;
      A meeting-place, an altar and a fire.

The Sword in the Sun

Angel: What is this about if not the Divine Identification with what you call 'Nature?' 'You saw His face in every flower,' did you not?

Me: I still think — in spite of myself — that only a 'religious' poem speaks of God. You are right of course, and I know it. I look at my brother, and I see Christ in him. This is what I must always seek to do, by Grace. But everything is my brother. May Hill is a fairy place, and the fairies — and Pan — are my brothers.

Angel: 'And the grass, alive and whispering.' It is only when you kill your vision by attempting to define it that 'pantheism' rears its ugly head. Sing to me again.

Me: What shall I sing? I hardly know what I have been writing about?

Angel: Tell me of your Uncle Willy's farm in Strath Braan. Sing to me of 'Tom na Gairn.'

Me: There is more that wells up from this black
  And bitter soil than that dark pool.
  Set upon a hill-top, bare of heather,
  Flanked by outposts of gray stones,
  Those waters, seeping from the blackest pit,
  Through moss and bog grass, here cascade
  Into another, smaller pool in tinkling clarity.

  A parable is this, perhaps a sacrament;
  The sorrow welling from the earth's deep core
  Here manifests in joy and light and gaiety .
  And on this hilltop, flanked by higher hills,
  Both being and becoming blend; the stillness
  Deep, impenetrable, alive with expectation.

  Now, set upon a great, gray rock,
  I see what eyes can see that, hauled
  Aloft by toiling feet, look far, far over

Divine Identification

Spreading heather, cairn and tumbled dike;
Yet looking further, somehow fail to see.
But that dark pool's a lens, a window
Waiting for a quiet eye's unhurried search
Within, to see within, and make therein discovery.

While toiling slowly to this height
Three tumbled farms I found;
A clachan on the hill, no more
Now than a scattering of round
Gray stones; by the burn
A roofless bothy, a stedding just
Discernible, a byre; and all now
In this same stillness, deep, impenetrable;
Stirred only by a breath of wind,
The distant fright of flighted grouse
And old ewes nosing for a mouthful.

Here fire had danced and given light
And worked expected, humble magic;
Contained by earth and fanned by air,
It heated water to the boil for broth
and brose and porridge. Domesticated elements

And humble magi, who in turn gave love
And consciousness, and mind and utterance;
Contained the welling sorrow in their hearts
And filtered it to bright cascade
In manifesting joy and gaiety.

Pipe and fiddle, dance and song,
Saga, story — all have gone.

The sorrow wells up dark in silent pools,
Deep from the black earth's broken heart.
"Tis there, upon that hill,' my aunt had said,
'I'm to be buried at the end.' I see her, arms
Floured white to the elbows, groaning table laid.
But when my uncle came in from the hill,
His blind eyes bright, and died upon the stair,
They buried him and carried her away.

The Sword in the Sun

The waters filter through the moss and stones,
Cascade at last in falls of light.
And my heart's ministry is what man's ever was;
Now set upon a gray rock, looking far,
Now close by crofter's fire in reverie —
To bring into that heart of love my consciousness,
Four elements, six senses, spirits and souls,
'Till being and becoming blend; and gathered in,
All things are glory, and are glorified; and all are one.

Angel: What is this about, other than the Divine Identification with
  Creation and man's priesthood?

Me: From God to God through man and through the rest of Creation?

Angel: Exactly so. Sing to me again. Sing of your little church and
  churchyard at Rudford.

Me: Once upon Eternity, under a changing sky
  When shadows moved, stirring the stillness of a stream
  Slow, slowly out of time; once, once where ley
  Lines swung upon a dance, and passing spirits passed
  From time, through timelessness, to time again;
  Once, here, the rough stones squared the ring
  And set the cross upon a crossing of the way,
  And nailed a blessing to this spot for me.

  Now, at the gray time of the river's rising,
  While spirits wait on trembling wing,
  The long-dead whisper at the great oak door.
  The waters of the wise wake, swirl and splash
  In their stone-set sea, and the gray stones sing;
  Rooks rise to the heavens and race in a ring
  To a changing sky from all change free
  Nobis quoque peccatoribus — Eternity!

Divine Identification

Once upon Eternity, 'when the Clerkes have dooen singing,
To saue and defend thy seruaunt our Kyng,'
Thy Angel over the wide waste winging
A stillness animate — shall shatter with light
The stream, the stones, the dance and the ring,
The changing sky and the great door's might,
Time, the long-dead, timelessness and me;
Redeem all, once, for all Eternity.

Angel: We have spoken of a *process* in things. You have it there in a
nutshell. You who overhear, sing your own songs! Look! Listen!
They rise within you and clamor to be sung.

The Sword in the Sun

iii

Angel: Let us again consider the Incarnation. With whom did our Lord identify?

Me: With fallen man. He identified the whole of the fallen human condition with Himself.

Angel: Is that all? What are the implications of such a Divine identification? I do not mean for man, I am thinking of other creatures.

Me: Through man, our Lord identified with the whole of life as it exists upon this wavelength. The whole of animal life is identified with Him, from man's physical body down to the minutest amoeba. It must be so. By becoming incarnate, by identifying with this wavelength, *the whole wavelength itself* must be identified with our Lord, *through man*.

Angel: And what are the implications of this?

Me: The mind boggles. Man is the summing-up of this wavelength. The evolution of Paleolithic man was Creation, on this wavelength, summing itself up. And all lower creatures are therefore in relationship with God through man, in addition to the direct relationships that might be theirs. But the implications of this for, let us say, the landscape as we know it — I cannot imagine.

The Sword in the Sun

Angel: Yes, the human mind does boggle. You cannot know all the implications now. But you have said a great deal, and more than you know. Why are you so worried about the landscape?

Me: Because of what Pan told me. I am sitting in my study in 'my world.' In his world, I am sitting in the middle of a lake. Now it is my world I am troubled about. It is this fallen world that is identified with this world through me, and which has brought my Paleolithic self to birth. What is to become of it?

Angel: It is not fallen, it is innocent. You fell from another plane of being and identified with this one. Your lower self is innocent. Do not project your fall upon an innocent world.

Me: I stand corrected. But what a puzzle! A world which is identified with God through me, by virtue of the Incarnation and yet innocent, and always God's world...

Angel: ...and never other than identified with Him. You and I and it abide forever *in God*.

Me: But are these two worlds Pan spoke of to remain forever separate? I have seen this lake, in my mind's eye, I think. I found myself on May Hill, and it was an island. All this was sea — or lake. And a friend said the other day that she could never take her shoes off in this house for fear of getting her feet wet! But not in this world, if you know what I mean. She *felt* the lake without knowing about it.

Angel: Yes, you did see it. And yes, she does feel it. And no, they will not remain separate. They will unite at the end of the age.

Me: That will be a catastrophe! And to my world, I think, not to Pan's. What of the animals?

Angel: Yes, a catastrophe; and yes, to your world and not to Pan's. And the animals? Why, they will all die.

Me: And then?

Angel: They will be forever alive, and you shall know them as they truly are, for you too shall be alive.

Me: And Pan's children? Will they transcend all such catastrophes as this? They are unfallen.

Angel: Yes; as Pan told you, 'They change, and change, and are changeless.' So shall you be, but according to a higher order.

The Sword in the Sun

iv

Angel: Now let us talk of Prayer once more. Sing to me again, little Brother. Tell me of the 'Atholl Brigade at Culloden!'

Me: Prayer? What has my piece of nationalist pride got to do with prayer? But no doubt you will tell me:

It is some comfort that, alone of all
The rightful line you, right of line,
Prevailed. When Keppoch fell and all was lost,
With Elcho's Life Guards and Fitzjames' Horse,
You, Campbell haunted on the flank,
Stood fast and stopped proud Hawley in his ride,
Held off the traitor and the Sassenach
Long, almost long enough — and died.

You ventured all for putting back the clock,
And held it still for one brief, glorious day —
And lost. Then long and bitter was its chime.
I wondered, as I stood beside your rock;
Were you, now Prince and King have passed away,
Perhaps two centuries before your time?

Angel: We are talking of Divine Identification. Your forefathers of the Atholl Brigade fell in battle. So did our Lord.

Me: You are not talking politics, that I know. You must mean the identification of a sacrifice of self for a cause sincerely believed in with our Lord's own sacrifice. In other words, having totally identified himself with man's fallen condition, all things — even wars can be turned into means of Grace. It matters less what happens than what man does with what happens.

Angel: Exactly! This age is passing and will soon be past. Wars have but a little time left before they cease forever. But there is no glorification of death in battle involved here; this is an identification of suffering, of sacrifice. And how do you know I am not talking politics? Is politics a forbidden subject for angels?

Me: It is an apparently forbidden subject for Bishops. Men always cry to the Church leaders for a lead, and then criticize them violently when they try to give one! But politics is a dirty business.

Angel: Politics is as dirty as those who practice it, and a community gets the politicians it deserves. But I am concerned with principle. Sing to me again; tell me of the Old Orchard.

Me: You bewilder me. Nevertheless:

> Here is my quiet corner, one might call it a glade,
> Tree and moss and wild-flower filled; here I
> Shall build my castle, there the stones shall be laid.
> So shall I raise it up to the leafy sky
> And reign there silent, sorrowful and sage,
> While mysteries are opened, magic made;
> While barren fruit-trees of advancing age
> Extend their frail embarrassment, and shade.
>
> Here, with a royal joy and an infinity of sorrow,
> These eyes will seek to blaze through stick and stone
> And, with the seer, see and see and know —
> And find that long-suspected thing was ever so.
> Here is my quiet corner, one might call it a throne,
> And here I reign today, and there tomorrow.

Divine Identification

Angel: Did you know what you were writing about, little Brother?

Me: Probably not. It was inspired by the far corner of the garden at Parkend Vicarage. The forest was on two sides; it was like a frontier post. I wanted to build a little hut for meditation and silence, and 'being myself' in. It seemed to be a kind of threshold to another world.

Angel: 'A royal joy and an infinity of sorrow.' Here is the Divine identification with your fallen world. And your quiet corner was a throne, and you 'reign' in your meditation, in your free will's attempt to identify with the Will of God. And tomorrow you shall indeed reign with Him; not here, but *there*.

Me: 'And find that long-suspected thing was ever so.' I did not realize, when I wrote it, that my poem was about Prayer.

Angel: All your poems are about Prayer, You define prayer far too narrowly. Sing to me of your 'Waiting.'

Me: Of all poems of mine, this, I should have thought, was the least prayerful. But here it is:

> Was it, perhaps, a subterranean saxophone,
> Two notes escaping to the open air?
> Or the passing scent of rich, expensive
> Cooking? Or the softly-spoken, liquid,
> Sensuous hiss of asphalt, tire-caressed
> In steady rain? Or was it, say,
> The flicker of the changing lights?
> Or the passing and the passing
> Of the twos and twos, shop-window lit,
> That brought this darkness on my mortal soul?
> She does not come! The mindless rain
> Falls on this smiling sensuality
> And falls the same within my NOW;
> My dark despair, my nightmare, my eternity.

Angel: The agony of separation; the pain of being incomplete; the ghastly void of 'my NOW; my dark despair, my nightmare, my eternity' — what is this but a microcosm of that human condition with which our Lord identified? The Bridegroom waits for his Bride. 'She does not come.' The agony is terrible and the Bridegroom bears it. All hurt young lovers are henceforth identified with Him in their agony. This poem is almost the most prayerful of all — if you want it to be!

Me: I suppose it is the 'smiling sensuality' that renders it 'irreligious.'

Angel: You and your horrible 'religion!' Is not God the Creator of the senses? Does he not require the fullest and most balanced sensuality? You identify too much with disease and not enough with health. And a 'religion' which encourages you to do this is itself diseased and needs much surgery.

Me: Were you a man and not an angel, you would be regarded by some as dangerously radical. And we are all too much tarred with this Manichaean brush. It accords ill with both the Gospel and the Risen Life which Christians are called to lead.

Angel: And our Lord is the most dangerous radical of all, and was crucified precisely because of it. So much for man-made 'religion!'

V

Angel: What is music, little Brother? Do you know?

Me: I love music, but how am I to define it? It is a pattern of sounds in two dimensions. There is melody and there is harmony; the horizontal and the vertical dimensions. And there is rhythm, which is almost a third dimension. The whole is, if you like, a vocabulary through which may be expressed great, emotional truths. But this is a bad start to a definition. I apologize, I am out of my depth.

Angel: Not so bad; but it is not the *truths* that are emotional, it is rather that they are emotionally perceived and expressed.

Me: I am persuaded that music — melody and harmony and rhythm — is expressive of the very being of God. It is the Creation in microcosm, and the character of the Mind in which Creation abides. But having said that, I hardly know what it is that I have said.

Angel: You are quite right, and yet you only know music upon one plane of existence. Is there music in a vacuum, little Brother?

Me: In so far as music depends upon sound waves through air; no there is not. But I have music in my head now. Music *is*. It cannot depend only upon the mechanics of its transmission.

The Sword in the Sun

Angel: No, it does not solely depend upon this. Tell me of the music that you have heard that does not so depend.

Me: I have heard the mountains singing when I stood at the top of the pass leading from the head of Glen Quaich to Kenmore, by Loch Tay. And I have heard fairy music by the waterfall at the Hermitage in Strath Braan. Both these dimensions of music were 'other.' I heard them, I think, with a different sense of hearing. And so did the others who were with me.

Angel: There is nothing in Creation that does not sing. And the whole of Creation is dancing. The Universe is the Great Dance, and our Lord is the Lord of the Dance. This you know already, for I myself have told you.

vi

Me: I am unsatisfied by what we said about music. It did not seem to get anywhere, and as our subject is 'the Divine Identification,' it did not seem to touch upon it.

Angel: Music is too deep a mystery for man to probe satisfactorily. But consider how its technique has developed in three centuries. Here is a full range of autumn colors indeed.

Me: Autumn colors? The autumn of what? The cycle of redemption; the age between the Incarnation and the Second Coming?

Angel: Yes, indeed! There is more to music than you can ever imagine. I, an angel, *am* music. I am made of music, and did you but know it, so are you.

Me: Then music as we know it is a kind of manifestation, an externalization, of the essence of our own being? And because man is priest to Creation, the harmony, and counterpoint, and melody and rhythm are expressions of the Creation glorifying God through man. Composition and performance — and appreciative enjoyment of music too — are an extension of Man's priesthood. The very essence of things is picked out and expressed in music. Am I right, or is this too fantastic?

Angel: You are quite right. Composition, performance and appreciation of music is always a worshipful and a priestly activity.

Me: But what about bad music? What about the shallow, popular music which does not last, and which palls almost as soon as it finds favor? Is that a worshipful, priestly affair?

Angel: Yes, at a primitive level. But do not despise it; it has its part to play. God created fleas as well as elephants.

Me: But the Divine Identification? The Mind of God is music; He is the fulfillment of harmony, melody, rhythm and so on. The whole Creation fulfills this potential — or seeks to fulfill it. The Divine Identification is in the very nature of things, for all things abide in God. And yet man's priesthood gives *particular expression* to the nature of things and they find a conscious expression of their adoration of God through man. And music is one aspect — an important aspect — of man's priesthood.

Angel: You have it! And now we will let our hearers make what they can of this. Perhaps there is an atheist among them; a musician who is startled and annoyed to find himself a priest of the Most High God! He shall be blessed.

vii

Angel: It is time for more poetry. What is poetry, little Brother?

Me: Poetry is 'emotion recollected in tranquillity,' according to Wordsworth. I fancy he is right, but I think it has a similar quality to music. I believe that it *is* music, rationally stated as it were.

Angel: Then let us have some. Tell me of your Native Land.

Me: The Whore of Babylon it is
That keeps the two of us apart!
A monstrous idol of a thing
That slave-men call 'Economy.'
And so you must remain far off;
An image of that state from which
I am forever exile; a dream
Of that with which I would identify,
And do identify, clapping about me
This after that, as if to wear
About my body that which dwells,
Yet unrequited, in my heart.

What is this thing you are?
What is that essence which,
Embracing and including all,
Finds its expression in those dreams
That haunt and hurt my memory?

You are not human. I discern
Strange, silent, elemental things;
Perchance a king of Devic kings,
A multitude of little states
In which abide spirits of wood
And water, flower and field, and stone,
In deep and wonderful embrace.

I have heard their music on the mountain tops
And have had a grave and silent commerce
With the great, gray stones
Who guard your secret kingdoms.
I have turned my careless feet away;
Whispered a blessing and been blessed.

This undefined, this enigmatic thing;
This, your essential being, I would wed,
As those have wed who shine
About your holy places, and have wound
Themselves and you about that golden thread
Which holds his jewels on their maker's head;
His crown, and our eternity.

Angel: You are a Scot, for all the English blood that is also in you. Tell me, what constitutes the essence of Scotland? Does it depend upon the people?

Me: No. It is the land itself. 'I discern strange, silent, elemental things.' The people conform to the land, it is that 'elemental something' which has welded together Pict, Scot, Anglo-Saxon and Briton into an unmistakable whole. We are heirs to a 'continuing something,' but I wish I knew what it was.

Angel: The Jews in the Old Testament thought it was an angel. Michael was believed to be the guardian of Israel.

Me: But the Jews have always had an identity apart from the land which they inhabit. No doubt it derives from it. Jerusalem, for them, is 'an image of that state from which I am forever exile;' but religion, not country, has held them together through all their dispersions.

Angel: Yes, the Jews are a special case, but it took great catastrophe to shake them loose from the *natural* identity with Palestine, into a *supernatural* identity with the religion that has been given them, and which remains their distinctive vocation. They are a reproach and a continuing object-lesson for Christians!

Me: In that the Christian faith transcends all natural identities and unifies men in the dispensation of Grace rather than that of Nature? But we will not have it. We must have our little divisions'.

Angel: Exactly. But whereas Grace completes and fulfills Nature, and brings all national identities into a unity, while maintaining the integrity of each, the *supernatural* identity of the Jewish people — not quite the same thing as Grace — separates them from natural and national identities. The Jew must stand apart; the Christian must transcend all. This is the vocation of each.

Me: But we have still not arrived at the identity of the 'something' which is the archetype of that thing which is the essence of Scotland. Is it elemental, or is it angelic, or is it something else? Or is it not profitable to ask?

Angel: It is angelic, but it is not profitable to pursue the matter further.

Me: I fancy that an awareness of national identity is essential to man's well-being, both individual and collective. Am I right?

The Sword in the Sun

Angel: Indeed you are! The denial to a race of their identity by a
more powerful governing race gives rise to 'Nationalism' which
can be very unbalanced. Sooner or later there is an explosion.
The loss of a sense of national identity is a most alarming sign
of decadence and must lead to disintegration and disorder. This
is the lot of all 'imperial' races; the higher you rise, the lower
you fall. This is only fair and reasonable. Men were not created
by God to exploit and dominate each other. But it is time for
more poetry. You took your son out for the day when he was at
preparatory school. You spent a little time in the church of St.
Mary Magdalene in Taunton. Tell me about it.

Me: Here is that thing called England;
    Intangible, elemental, quiet.
    Here the very earth soars up,
    Pillared and arched and many-aisled,
    To roof us over in great stillness
    And fill the air with quiet music —
    Rustic, English as the pews we sit in;
    Not made for over-much devotion.

    We walked to the car through darkening streets,
     Shop windows lit and a cold wind blowing;
    Moving more deeply through the littered land,
    At Peace — and yet troubled and wondering.
    The boy paused, and ruffled the cap on his head;
    'I could have stayed there for ever,' he said.

Angel: Your English blood rose to the surface on that occasion. Let
us leave the matter there for the time being.

viii

Angel: Tell me about the Divine Identification with nations, little Brother. Do not look startled, we shall not concern ourselves with power-politics!

Me: This is a two-fold identification. In the first place there is the essence of the thing itself; an angelic principle which governs the landscape, to which the elementals conform, and which provides what, for want of a better word, I will call the 'atmosphere' — the *character* is a better word still. Am I right so far?

Angel: Yes, go on.

Me: In the second place there is the human identification with the countryside. This is a long-term development, but perhaps not so long term as we suppose. Two or three generations might suffice, as the former British Dominions bear witness.

Angel: Yes; your Canadian relations were wholly Highland Scots four generations ago. Now they are wholly Canadian and Scotland is a foreign country to them. Go on.

Me: But the Divine Identification with nations is through man's own identification. Each national character is taken up to become a part of the fullness of Man in Man's fulfillment. Again, that with which man has identified is of God — angelically and elementally constructed. This whole business of nationality is a part of man's priesthood to Creation. It can be nothing else in the last resort, but I shudder to think of the way that priesthood is spoiled.

Angel: And now fit reincarnation into your pattern.

Me: This is but another dimension. A new dimension to the soul: a European subjugating India in one life, and an Indian undergoing the process and hating it in the next! It is a poetic idea, and love may well require it, but I think the important point is the wholeness of the humanity found in a man who has consciously identified with many nations. This adds depth to his priesthood. It may not be necessary, in Christ, but it must surely be an enrichment?

Angel: It is not necessary, in Christ. It is a realizing of an enrichment already given. In Christ, all men are made whole, there is no particular value in having lived in many nations, for in Heaven man experiences the unity of all. I set a little trap for you; it nearly caught you.

Me: There is no lack in any man Baptized into Christ. All will be fulfilled, and the fulfillment is inherent in the Baptism; but there is a certain poetry, I think, in the realizations by a man, for love's sake, of a tiny part of that which has been freely given him. But this is of this age only, and the age is nearly past. We have been thinking of Divine Identification, but again and again we return to the fact that all things abide in God, and that man's priesthood is a new dimension, a new means of Grace to man and to Creation, born of the fall of man and man's redemption.

Angel: Yes, and there we will leave it. The mystery is so deep that we may probe it for ever, and indeed in Heaven you shall. It shall be your Joy. You who overhear; it shall be your Joy too.

The Wheel Ascends

i

Angel: Some of your friends like to talk of the 'Evolution of God;' others proclaim that 'God is dead!' What do you make of these ideas, little Brother?

Me: I am bound to say that they both fail to make any sense at all. I think we have dealt with the idea of the Evolution of God by saying that the Mind of God, in which all things abide, is a living Mind full of living thoughts. God is dynamic. Evolution is a subjective, human term for *our* experience of *his* dynamism. Long words! I suspect them. The longer the words, the greater the nonsense as a rule. Am I right so far?

Angel: Quite right so far. Now what of the 'death of God?'

Me: This is the death of false concepts of God and is to be welcomed. The idea of God as a 'stop-gap' for the holes in our knowledge is grotesque. It is as if a motorist who knew nothing about the mechanics of his motor car, explained its breakdown by saying 'God is dead,' and pointing to the engine. It is the terrible naiveté behind the learned expositions of the 'death of God' idea that alarms me. I suspect an unbalanced, sentimental transcendentalism behind it. Long words again. But who, having a living, personal relationship with our Lord in prayer and Sacraments can possibly *mean* what they write about this? I suspect much of this is a clever 'front' for mere human cleverness. I am being unkind and critical; I must stop.

Angel: And you must also stop making sweeping statements! But I can pick pieces of truth out of what you have said which, when cleaned up, will do very well!

Me: And what am I to say to that? I deserved it.

Angel: We have given ourselves a subject: *The Wheel Ascends*. Tell me, little Brother, what wheel; and where is it going?

Me: Having set the title of our conversation, you now ask me to make sense of it for you! Very well, I will do what I can. The 'Wheel' is, I take it, the 'Wheel of Life' about which we had some discussion earlier. Where is it going? Well, upwards, I suppose! But you will ask me to elaborate, will you not? I will hazard a guess that the Wheel of Life is in process of *evolution,* but only subjectively, however objective the process may be to us.

Angel: Now please tell me what you mean by that.

Me: I hardly know! But let me try to bring my thoughts together. The Wheel of Life, in all its forms and however it is understood, is about to change with the coming of the New Age. You have used the word 'ascends' and so I am bound to think of an evolutionary process taking place. But God is unchanging, and so he is not affected by this — he is not to be altered! Therefore it is all within his own thoughts; subjective to God, objective to us who abide in his thoughts. I have done no more than repeat myself. I am out of my depth.

Angel: Do you deny God the right to change his mind? Your Old Testament is full of stories of God 'repenting him of the evil,' and withholding his wrath.

Me: But these are anthropomorphisms. They are naive as far as a doctrine of God is concerned. Surely we know better now?

Angel: I had no idea that you were the Almighty! I do beg your pardon!

Me: Yes, I had my tongue in my cheek. Man is made in God's image and therefore man can relate himself to God and God to himself; and more than ever since the Incarnation. But I still think that those Old Testament stories of God 'repenting him of the evil' are a naive mode of expression.

Angel: May not God change his mind?

Me: Who am I to say no? My difficulty resides, I believe, in the fact that mind-changing, in human terms, is so often a sign of vacillation, of indecision, of self-interest. I fancy, too, that St. Thomas Aquinas has said, somewhere, that God never changes his mind. It may not be St. Thomas Aquinas at all, but I half-remember a 'stock quotation' from my theological college days. I am inhibited; that is my trouble.

Angel: Never mind about St. Thomas Aquinas! He was big enough to change his mind. He described all his massive scholarship as 'so much straw!' Your really great men always change their minds because they are big enough to do so. It is the little mind that cannot bear to change. You know that as well as I do. And has not Love compelled you to change your mind, over and over again?

Me: Then it is basic to the very nature of 'mind' that it changes?

Angel: Of course it is! Will you fill God's head with concrete, or 'set' his thoughts like a hard-boiled egg? Have you not observed my dealings with you? 'Mind' is *personal* and is always reacting afresh to persons. Is God less than his creatures in this? I tell you that He changes his Mind all the time. Call that 'evolution' if you like, but you men make evolution sound a very mechanical process, whereas it is nothing of the kind. It moves by fits and starts. It does what seems profitable, and then it 'changes its mind' and does something else. That is why it is such a puzzle to you. But the main drift of events remains constant, and the *Character* is unalterable. Note that Character! One of its constituent parts is the very archetypal sense of Fun!

Me: We are always trying to reduce God to the level of a machine. We abdicate our own manhood to computers; soon we shall fall down and worship them, I fear.

Angel: Already you do, and it is your ruin. Little do you know what you are doing, for as soon as the life of man loses its personal quality, it is no longer life. It is death animated. Look at your cities and think! Our hearers; look, and think too!

ii

Angel: Let us return to poetry. Sing to me of the Bridegroom's
Footsteps, little Brother.

Me: It is a waiting there;
Waiting, uncertain, in the forest shade,
Chilled by the cold night air.
The mist that clings to the dark rock
Chills with a sudden breath of smoke,
And the climb is a groping into darkness

With the dreaded image of the gray man
Flashed on the mind's bare wall.
Cold fingers clutch at the protecting sheet
And tremble in both fear and adoration
At the sounds of the bridegroom's footsteps;
Seeing the door handle turn in the silence.

See how, from these steep and soaring heights
Falling as a golden spear
Towards the quarry's heart,
The angels and the holy ones
Pour out the blessed song of silence
And wash away the bounds of time;

And see, the mists are clearing
From off the distant hills;
Spear upon each gleaming spear
As timeless comes the day,
And the long call of the trumpet
Sings clear across the firmament.

The Sword in the Sun

Now comes he to his garden
In the blue of morning?
Age flowering into age
And orbit into orbit,
And all the teeming sounds of silence
Hanging by a golden thread?

Angel: What is that about, little Brother?

Me: I hardly know. I wrote it while at theological college, while my
whole spiritual awareness was growing at a terrible pace. It
was part of a longer poem still, but I can only see in it an attempt to describe the almost fearful expectation I felt at our
Lord's nearness in prayer, and at the same time the awareness
of 'break-through' into the world beyond. But this is hard! If I
had known exactly what it was that I was trying to say I should
have written prose, not poetry.

Angel: Exactly! And it was unkind of me to ask you. But this is our
dilemma as we attempt to consider the ascent of the Wheel of
Life. There is a moving up into a new dimension. Scripture
tells you that Heaven and earth shall pass away, and there shall
be a new Heaven and a new earth. What can this mean? You
cannot imagine it. I can, but I cannot describe it to you. Let us
have another poem. You call it 'Being.'

Me: And an odd one it is. I do not understand it even now.

Tall trees cast long shadows
Which lie, illusions of a grand illusion.
The spring and summer of our lives, spent
Climbing the short, steep hill,

Prepare us for an incarnation;
And the dying fire carries our fire
Over the world's edge — while the trees
Become their shadows and vanish in the night.

Maya dies where the tall oak dies,
Stretching its long arms in the darkening sun;
Where the blood-red leaves perpetually fall

Redeeming the illusion. Karma dies
In incarnation, and illusion fades
Into existence with the rising sun.

Angel: Yes, it is odd, but it compelled itself to be written. You were not merely performing an exercise in versification when you wrote it.

Me: I don't know what to say. There are others that I wrote which tried to express dreams — the dreams that are not dreams if you understand me! I do not understand them, but they had to be written. The 'something' had to find expression.

Angel: Like 'Enigma?' Tell me of that, little Brother.

Me: The morning glitters on radiant bodies
Tumbling light in the sensuous surf;
Splashing music with such gleaming words
As ring, knife-edged, on the ice-clear air;
Responsaries from a lover to the loved.

The scales of time run side by side
Contained within their meeting point;
Short-circuiting on souls that dream.

Angel: And here you have the solution to the mystery. 'The scales of time run side by side contained within their meeting-point.' This is the simple truth and poetically it may be stated, but make an 'ism' of it and you reduce it to utter nonsense. There are two modes of perception of realities: the rational and the intuitive. The intuitive are the 'souls that dream,' and mystical experience is very like a short-circuit. In terms of simple fact those last three lines are well stated. You saw what shall be. It relates to what is, but it is 'wholly other.'

iii

Angel: It is time we turned to Holy Scripture, little Brother. What do you learn of the Coming Again in the New Testament?

Me: First of all I learn that it is quite firmly and specifically promised by our Lord. The Son of Man will be seen coming on the clouds of heaven — poetic language no doubt — and accompanied by his angels. His power and glory will be manifest.

Angel: Yes, poetic language, but you shall be very surprised! What does He say about the condition of the world before he comes?

Me: He speaks of wars, rumors of wars, civil dissensions, a breakdown in family life, natural catastrophe and every sign of disaster to man. The End will be quite catastrophic.

Angel: No, not the End itself; that will be glorious beyond man's imagination because it will be a Beginning to a life of infinite discovery. But the time before the End will be terrible.

Me: The lucky ones will be the ones who will be killed?

Angel: In a way, yes. But that is a negative way of looking at it. Every man has his own vocation. What did the early Church believe?

Me: The early Church believed — and passionately hoped — that the End would be soon; tomorrow, today, now! St. Paul had, on at least one occasion, to warn some Christians not to give up work, but to carry on normal lives. This was the measure of their hope. Paul's remarks to the Corinthian Christians about marriage must be seen in the light of this 'at any minute now' hope of the Second Coming.

Angel: And was the early Church wrong?

Me: Not at all. Except in their actual timing. The Resurrection and the Second Coming were all that mattered. Man was reconciled to God in Christ, death was defeated, 'the sky was the limit' and the sooner all was accomplished the better.

Angel: You are absolutely right. That *is* the Christian Faith in a nutshell. What do you make of the Church since those days?

Me: I want to say that she has fallen away terribly from her simple faith. But I cannot. The dramatic, urgent hope of the Second Coming faded, and the Church became an institution. She rapidly became institutionalized. This was inevitable, I think.

Angel: Yes, quite inevitable, and quite proper, go on.

Me: The Church 'lived dangerously' until the time of the Emperor Constantine. Her mission was evangelism — as it always is — and after the Peace of the Church which came with Constantine, her evangelistic work positively 'exploded' as most of the Empire was baptized. But I wonder! Was this genuine? How much sincerity was there in an 'Established' Church in those days?

Angel: Very much more than there is in an 'Established' Church now! It was the right development for the age. Abuses abounded, but overall it was right.

Me: As the years wore on, it seems to me that the hope of the Coming Again became almost extinct — stifled by institutionalism. We made an 'ism' of the institution and worshipped it. And then, the schism between East and West, and that nightmare called the Reformation. The outward unity of Christians was shattered, and war broke out between rival institutionalisms. Actual bloodshed very often. Power Politics and the Gospel, all muddled up together.

Angel: Did not St. John, on Patmos, tell you that the dragon would be released after a thousand years? His time is nearly up.

Me: Revelations is a very difficult book. It is a happy-hunting-ground for academics and madmen alike. It is hard to know what to make of it. It is poetry; the writer was describing the indescribable. He was describing what *was* when he wrote. Not all of it *is now*, but some of it *shall be*. Am I right?

Angel: Yes, roughly. Which are you, an academic or a madman?

Me: Neither, or both. I do not bracket the two together as a matter of course?

Angel: Our hearers must make their own minds up. I told you at the beginning that some would think you mad, little Brother. Let them return to their Bibles and read of the Coming Again.

The Sword in the Sun

iv

Angel: The Second Coming; how do you imagine it, little Brother?

Me: What a question! How can I imagine the unimaginable?

Angel: But you have seen.

Me: Yes, I have seen the unimaginable. I have seen the Holy Angels, but with a kind of 'other' vision. They related to my environment, but my environment seemed to 'fade away' where they were.

Angel: Go on.

Me: And I have been aware of human beings present, in a heavenly dimension, dancing at the place of their own Passion. One spoke to me, and I shall not forget her.

Angel: What was it you said in your poem? 'The scales of time run side by side, contained within their meeting-point.' You were identified with that meeting-point. You say they 'short-circuit' in souls that dream. So they do, but at the End it will be no short-circuit; their 'meeting point' will Himself manifest and the unimaginable will have occurred, and men will wonder why they ever found it difficult to imagine.

The Sword in the Sun

The Wheel Ascends

V

Angel: It is time for poetry again. You say more than you know in your poems, little Brother.

Me: So it seems! I had no idea, when I wrote them, of the use to which they would be put.

Angel: And if you had known, the poems would have been useless. But I was looking over your shoulder when you wrote them. I did not write them for you, but I am your guardian angel! Tell me of 'an Exorcism.'

Me: 'I hope you won't be shocked,' she said
    With honest eyes, twisting her gloves
    Between unconscious, nervous hands.
    There is no shocking any more;

    All pain is gathered up, all borne
    In one eternal painfulness;
    The universe a running sore
    Made whole, the iron bands

    That bound it, broke; all loves
    Made one in Love; all dead,
    Alive. The good and evil twist
    And turn within the exorcist

    'Till with Christ's love his heart runs red.
    'I hope you won't be shocked,' she said.

The Sword in the Sun

Angel: That girl had dignity and your compassion was aroused by it. She did not conceal the shame she felt. She was utterly honest and you, a priest, loved her for it. So does God love man. So he changed his Mind, just as you changed your mind. He responded, just as you responded. God is not a machine, and neither are you.

Me: You have made your point — with me at any rate.

Angel: Excellent! Now tell me of 'The River.'

Me: I cast a stick into a stream
  And saw it, slowly turning, turn
  To dust upon another shore,
  From whence will grow one day an oak;
  And there will come another man
  And pull a stick
  To cast it down into the stream
  And see it, slowly turning, turn
  To dust.

  Look deep with me into this stone
  And see its substance open wide;
  A universe of stars, all insubstantial;
  A potency becoming act by deep
  Immutable intent. Look deep
  Into this river, see it fade
  Into a frosty winter's night.
  Look for the Polestar.
  Look for light.

  Thus do we seem
  To stand upon a state of mind,
  A starlit sky
  Of no known substance, only thought;
  Myself an idea, you a dream.

Angel: That is all we need say just now. Thank you, little Brother.

vi

Angel: The Bible again! How does St. John describe our Lord?

Me: Is it a learned volume you want, or a simple answer? And how to give a simple answer.? I will try to be brief by saying that St. John slightly corrects the picture given in the Synoptic Gospels (i.e.: Matthew, Mark and Luke) and uses language that reflects the philosophical ideas of the Greek world. He uses 'Platonic' ideas — scholars argue about this and about the significance of this — but there is no doubt that he presents our Lord in a way that the non-Jewish world would have found meaningful.

Angel: What do you mean by 'Platonic' ideas?

Me: Plato had a doctrine that there is a 'perfect' world of archetypes or 'forms,' of which this world is an imperfect replica. St. John presents our Lord as belonging to this perfect world — i.e.: Heaven. 'I am from above, you are from below.' This theme runs all through his work. It is a considerable development of Plato's ideas, but it would be meaningful to a non-Jewish world.

Angel: Why?

Me: Because the Jew's concerns were with *morals*, and the Greek's concerns were with *metaphysics*. The Fall, a Jewish concern, is a moral problem. The imperfection of this world is, to the Greeks, a philosophical problem. St. John bridged that gap. He presented

Jesus in both moral and metaphysical terms. Our Lord, the God-man from the perfect world of archetypes, has bridged the gap between the perfect and the imperfect worlds, and has begun the process of their identification; their union. Is that a satisfactory answer?

Angel: Yes, good enough for our purpose. Our Lord has bridged the gap, the cycle of identification is nearly complete.

Me: But has St. John put Greek words into our Lord's mouth? Some scholars doubt that the Fourth Gospel contains the exact words of the Christ. They are very different from his words as reported in the Synoptic Gospels.

Angel: Scholars will doubt anything; it is their trade! Was our Lord ignorant of the whole drift of non-Jewish thinking in a very mixed society? Were the contents of the four Gospels his only utterances in three years ministry? Why, you yourself run through a Gospel's length of chatter in an evening among friends! And if St. John set out to correct an unbalanced picture, is it surprising that his correction is different? And had you only the Fourth Gospel, someone would have had to have produced the Synoptic Gospels as a corrective! Rejoice in the balance of what you have.

Me: Our Lord bridged two gaps between Heaven and earth. He bridged the moral gap by identifying man's fallen state with Himself. And he bridged the metaphysical gap between Heaven and earth by becoming incarnate — the very thing which bridged the moral gap. And the 'bridge' could only be built from the Heavenly shore, not the earthly.

Angel: But what are morals and metaphysics?

Me: Subjective human attempts to give expression to a mystical experience. The mystically perceived reality is objective; man's subjective response is a moral, person-to-person one, and a metaphysical, rationally understood one. But the Reality transcends both. And here I am using just those long words you complained about earlier. And at your bidding!

Angel: I wanted to give you a chance to show how clever you are, little Brother!

The Sword in the Sun

vii

Angel: It is time for some more poetry. Sing to me of 'Indigo Un-
heralded!'

Me: It is a strange, disquieting discovery; almost
 Embarrassing as if, abroad with hat and coat
 And dogs on leash, we stumbled on
 The mouth of Hell, mumbled apology
 And hurried on. This crater lies
 In forest silence, out of business now;
 Inhabited by ghosts and memories
 Who, if we're quiet, are not disturbed by us.

 The crater curves from crumbling lips
 To sudden silence and the night of time.
 The stone-lined darkness of an ancient shaft
 Utters a deep, compelling call;
 Evokes not past, but present; speaks
 Of paths to follow, not to fall.

Angel: What is it about, little Brother?

Me: It is about an old pit-shaft, deep inside the Forest, near where
I used to live. The mouth of the shaft was choked with branches
and leaves, but I always felt that a great chasm yawned beneath it. I was much interested in the Qabalah at that time,
and was reminded of the 'thirty-second path,' meditation upon
which led the consciousness into parts of the unconscious mind.

This shaft into the 'within' of earth — physically, I mean —
evoked these ideas very strongly.

Angel: But why the 'mouth of Hell?'

Me: I hardly know. It seemed an apt description at the time. There
was unknown peril, a hint of menace, and certain death if I had
in fact jumped down the shaft. There is something about the
middle of the earth which is, somehow, alarming. One does not
know what might emerge from the depths.

Angel: No, you do not! There is more behind that unease than you
suppose. Now sing to me again — of 'Tewkesbury Abbey.'

Me: I am fey, so they say;
    I have seen the walking dead
    Hurry to Mass on a weekday morning.
    I have heard the doors go bang
    And have heard their footsteps hurrying.
    I have heard the solemn warning
    Through and beyond the bell's wild clang;
    The long, clear call from the tower.

    A time and times pass all in one;
    The tall stone pillars see, and nod
    And see again, and feel a stir
    And sense that something must occur
    Concerning them, and men, and God.
    Signs in the moon and in the sun.

Angel: What solemn warning was this?

Me: It was a long trumpet-blast which seemed to come, one evening,
from the top of the tower. I was reminded that 'the trumpet
shall sound and we shall be changed!' Afterwards, I told myself

that it was a barge siren from the river and that I was imagining things.

Angel: No, it was not a barge siren. It began the whole process of thought in you which has brought you to this moment. It awoke in you a sense that 'something must occur,' and that there were indeed 'signs in the moon and in the sun.'

Me: It awoke in me an eschatological hope, you mean?

Angel: You and your long words! It reminded you of the Second Coming. 'The long, clear call from the tower' was for you what, in your army days, you would have called a 'warning order.' But it was not just for you. You who overhear; it was for you as well!

The Sword in the Sun

viii

Angel: The Wheel Ascends! What do you make of this, little Brother?

Me: Nothing very 'concrete,' but a great deal in a vague, intuitive, half-perceived and less-than-half understood sort of way.

Angel: That is splendidly clear! Give some examples.

Me: First of all I am clear that the cycle of redemption, begun at our Lord's Incarnation and to be fulfilled at his Coming Again, is not merely another 'turn of the wheel' as it were. God is a Person — he is the source of all 'personhood' — and he *reacts*. His thoughts develop, his Mind is original, and the development of his thoughts often takes an original turn. He changes his Mind! His Mind never acts out of character, the end products are never forsaken, but the very *concept* of them develops — they put on new dimensions. So it has been, and so it is, and so it shall be, with man.

Angel: Excellent! But what is the cause of your difficulties in understanding?

Me: There are two causes. The first is the limitations of this world. A mortal, fallen mind cannot stretch far. The second is fundamental: I am a thought in the Mind of God! I am *undergoing* development and revision within that Mind. I cannot view either the Mind in which I am a thought objectively, nor myself as I understand myself objectively. My very being is in a state of flux! It is eternally secure in the Love of God, but not by any means a 'fixed' or 'static' thing. I have nowhere to put my feet.

Angel: Except upon the certainty of the Love of God. What else do you perceive?

Me: I am aware that the cycle is drawing to an end, that the Coming Again, long neglected by the Church as her greatest hope, is closer than any of us can imagine. I have received a 'warning order' these ten years since, and the conviction that a New Age is about to dawn is growing steadily within me, and ever more urgently.

Angel: And that is as much as you can put into words, little Brother. Our hearers; think on these things!

The Moment of Truth

The Moment of Truth

i

Angel: The moment of truth, little Brother! What does this suggest to you?

Me: The sudden, expected, yet wholly unexpected return of the Christ in glory. Suddenly all men will see things as they are and will know themselves for what they are because they will see Him as he is.

Angel: A Great Assize?

Me: Yes. But I don't think that this courtroom imagery is as helpful to us as it might have been to a former generation. I don't imagine our Lord as a county court judge. I fancy the judgments will have become an integral part of each person's being. I fancy that we judge ourselves. Love, not law, is the criterion.

Angel: Yes. Love, not law, is the criterion. And judgment is indeed self-inflicted. But our Lord is not passive. You know, because you have experienced it, that he for Love's sake may cancel out the sentence of destruction you pass upon yourself and restore you wholly. He is the Lord.

Me: And does this work the other way round? Surely not.

Angel: No, he will not destroy a clear conscience. But think it possible that for Love's sake he may allow a self-imposed sentence of destruction to stand.

Me: For Love's sake? How?

Angel: There may be those for whom Heaven would be an eternal Hell!

Me: Then we are masters of our own ultimate destiny?

Angel: Absolutely!

ii

Angel: It is time for some more poetry. Tell me of the 'Joy in Heaven.'

Me: They were angry when we walked across their grave
And followed us. They led us to their room
And took their places, set each on a chair
Where they had sat, four hundred bitter years,
And filled both house and garden with despair.

And so the four of us held parliament,
And street lights cast long shadows on the floor,
'Till love broke through four centuries of pride
And brought them down to lay their secrets bare;
To tell his murder, tell her suicide.

Melchizedek, he brought forth bread and wine
For priest he was, and pleading as he did,
The host of heaven rode in upon the rite,
Set flame about that still, that silent pair,
And bore them homeward on a blaze of light.

Angel: When was the moment of truth for those two ghosts to whom
you ministered, little Brother?

Me: I think there were two moments of truth in each case. In the
case of the murderer, it was first the moment of consent to the
temptation to commit the grave sin — a sin against his own
integrity as well as against his victim. Second, the moment of

truth — the real one — was the solemn facing of that fact in penitence after four hundred years. For the suicide it was much the same. Earthly death had not radically altered their situation.

Angel: Yes, fall and redemption all over again. But the ultimate moment of truth was ...?

Me: The moment of redemption, when the host of heaven 'bore them homeward on a blaze of light.'

Angel: Exactly! Now sing to me again — of the 'Monks of Tewkesesbury. '

Me: And now, my friends in Paradise
(For here is part of Paradise),
As my time comes to go,
A part of me remains with you
To stand on vanished *statio*
And go, in God, to the Work of God.
Benedicamus Domino.

Comrades in love are you and I;
It shall continue so
Until I stand entire at last
Who now, on either side of death,
Sing the eternal Hours that pass.
There are no more farewells in Christ.
Deo Gratias.

Angel: And the moment of truth for them?

Me: It *is*, perpetually.

Angel: Exactly!

iii

Angel: Reconcile for me the ideas of universal salvation and eternal damnation, little Brother!

Me: I had hoped that you would do this for me. However, I will do my best. It is the will of God that all his creatures shall live. Our Lord came to save *all men*. Universal salvation is the *desire* of God, but God has given man free-will, and he will respect it to the very end. If it is the whole tenor of a man's free will that he perish, then, although I cannot imagine such a thing, I am bound to conclude that perish he will. I cannot imagine God destroying a man who, at the last, *wanted* to live and be with Him eternally.

Angel: Go on.

Me: Only God knows who are really 'his own.' Only he knows the true state of a man's will. At the moment of truth, both will know — clearly — and there will be complete agreement between them. And God's love for the damned will be infinite.

Angel: Yes, indeed it will. But if his Love for them is infinite, must they not continue, in some way, to abide in that Love?

Me: Here is the puzzle! How can they abide? As the memory of a failure? Is this a failure of God's?

Angel: You men completely misunderstand failure. You identify success and failure with your own personal pride, and you are quite unable to be dispassionate and objective about them. God has no 'personal pride.' He is wholly dispassionate, and wholly objective. This is perfect Love.

Me: Then God accepts failure? But it is not a failure of his Love, it is the failure of the creature to respond to it. And the creature has been given the autonomy which makes failure inherently possible.

Angel: Yes, that inherent possibility is part of the creature's dignity.

Me: But how can something that has lost its being continue to *abide*?

Angel: You ask me? You have already been through that experience! You were destroyed. You abode long, long in the memory of God. And then He changed his Mind.

iv

Angel: Let us talk of Prayer. What of the moment of truth in that context, little Brother?

Me: I can only speak of what I know. The moment of truth was, for me, the confrontation with our Lord in person that I spoke of earlier. I saw Him — that is to say, I was overpoweringly aware of his Presence and his Holiness. I saw the truth about myself, and I saw and *knew* the truth about the Redemption. *My* redemption! The moment of truth, in prayer, is the confrontation with the Christ *in person*. But it happens very differently to each person, each according to his need.

Angel: Yes, to each according to his need. No man was ever converted by argument. It is always a personal confrontation, in some form or another, which converts or repels a man.

Me: Repels? I cannot imagine it!

Angel: Nevertheless, sometimes it is so. It must be so, at least in theory, if man has a free will. And sometimes it is so in practice as well.

Me: I am trying to frame a question about integrity, but I find it hard. Might it be central to a man's integrity that he be repelled? I can't think of such a one, but is it possible?

Angel: No, it is not possible. It is the moment of *Truth*, not of man's illusions and misunderstandings.

175

The Sword in the Sun

V

Angel: Sing to me again, little Brother. Sing to me of 'Wester Ross.'

Me: When I was a wild, romantic loon
　　　I dreamed of climbing high and higher hills
　　　'Till, set at last upon a sheer and lonely crag,
　　　I'd pitch my tent and, sudden vision-rent,
　　　I'd write my revelations, and then die.

　　　I'm older now; I would not start so soon
　　　Upon my quest, for cold, not vision, kills!
　　　And I'll not lightly, for romance or rag,
　　　Burst in upon a silence, heaven-sent,
　　　That lies between those mountains and the sky.

　　　I'll learn my notes before I play a tune,
　　　Content to lift mine eyes unto the hills
　　　(Identified thus more than any stag),
　　　Revitalising thence this life I'm lent;
　　　Uniting them all with me when I die.

Angel: The moment of truth...where is it here?

Me: The moment of union with those hills when I find them
　　　in God.

Angel: And the rest of the poem?

Me: The process of growing up! Of becoming that man who can find them in God at the end, and whose love is such that he will find them.

Angel: The process of learning to know where to look for them. Now sing to me again. Tell me of 'Separation.'

Me: I have a go-between with you;
    One who unites in separation.
    One whom our love is in and through
    And who effects its consecration;

    Who's love-life with the Father is
    The Real, of which our's is the toy
    Who's antic jerk and clockwork whizz
    Analogies the Heavenly Joy.

    This flesh, wrapped in the lonely sheet,
    Is but addition to the soul's idea In God.
    Why then!! We two do meet
    In Him this night, this night my dear.

Angel: As with things, so with persons — except that all things are persons. Did you realize when you wrote it, that that poem transcended life and death, little Brother?

vi

Angel: Ask Pan, little Brother, about the moment of truth.

Me: He is here? Pan, my Brother in Christ, what is the moment of truth to you? What does this mean to you?

Pan: It is now, little Brother; it is all the time; it is everywhere.

Me: What do you think of the moment of truth as far as men are concerned?

Pan: I do not understand.

Me: What do you think of mankind, Pan?

Pan: I do not know what to think. They are all mad, yet not all.

Me: What do you think will become of us?

Pan: I fear lest you perish. You destroy your own earth.

Angel: And that will be the moment of truth indeed!

Me: I fear lest we destroy Pan's world as well as our own.

Pan: You cannot destroy that which is. You can only destroy that which is not.

Angel: Our hearers, think on these things!

vii

Angel: Sing to me again, little Brother. Tell me of 'Utopia.'

Me: There is no glory in it now;
    Great days are over and the rest
    Are passing, and the point is gone.
    There are no noble causes left to die for,
    No inequalities to mend. Today
    All things are uniformly gray.

    Endeavour's past; there's no way now.
    Invention's smothered, and the best
    Is fled. The dull-eyed mass go dully on,
    Their future blank, their present dead,
             their past alone to cry for;
    One object stamped on each stale breath:
    Orgasm, oblivion, and an early death.

Angel: What does this describe?

Me: It describes my own times. All the hopes of 'a brave new world,'
    and 'welfare states,' and world peace and harmony have all gone
    stale. There is no outlet for endeavor. It is a cry of frustration.

Angel: It is a song of old age — the end of an age. It is a death wish.
    Sing to me of 'Nirvana Point,' little Brother.

Me: Becoming is a falling;
A falling out of knowledge into darkness.
Darkness is not the negation of light
But a condition of it. As darkness grows
So grows the knowing which is love;
The true knowing, growing as the being shrinks
And journeys to Nirvana Point;
The end of all becoming.

Our being falls towards this point
Where all the lines converge
And funnels terminate.
Nirvana Point, shaped like a cross;
The spinning coin whose heads is light
And tails darkness. The lens and shutter
Of the cosmic camera, whose fitful click
Flashes an image on the soul's pin-point
As it hurtles down in its light tight box.

Alpha and Omega. We fall from one
Towards the other, our antipodes.
Pilgrims, we pass the iron gates
Of our Nirvana, where becoming
Is fulfilled; where falling turns
To soaring, in the one straight line
Alpha to Omega; and both are one.

Angel: There are two ways of looking at things. The first was subjective and negative; the second, objective and positive. Here is
your Hope, little Brother!

viii

Angel: What of the moment of Truth, little Brother?

Me: It is the confrontation with the Christ; the discovery of all that we have been and have loved in Him.

Angel: Go on.

Me: It is the moment of total accord with the Truth Himself, either for Life or destruction. It is the fulfillment, the consummation, of the whole tenor of our being, as we have chosen to use that being.

Angel: It is the moment when Love finds its ultimate expression, for acceptance or rejection by man.

Me: And that moment is the summing-up of many moments.

Angel: And after that summing-up, there is no more to be said.

The Sword in the Sun

The Parting of the Ways

The Parting of the Ways

i

Angel: Little Brother; tell me of the parting of the ways.

Me: There seems little to tell. Soon, our Lord will Come Again; soon the moment of Truth will have arrived. And that moment is the parting of the ways. There are only two possible ways to go: onwards, or out.

Angel: So it shall be. Holy Scripture contains it all.

Me: But, Brother; what of the devil at the End?

Angel: Pray for him lest he perish utterly. The rest is not your business.

Me: What remains to be said?

Angel: Another poem for good measure. Sing to me of a blessed place. Tell me of 'Ardnamurchan.'

Me: I do not know what made me climb that hill,
    As if to round off forty years with one
    Short burst of trite, symbolic energy.
    Did I expect a crossroads at the summit?
    Or a clear call to irreversible decision?

    I do not know. But when I stood
    Upon the topmost rock there was no more

The Sword in the Sun

A world before my feet. All, all was flame.
A sea of fire like molten glass from
This world's end, upon whose very edge
I stood, spread out, and all was flame.
My road, its crossroads far behind,
Had ended now. And all was now
And fire; and only now and fire remained.

Angel: Yes, little Brother. Only now and fire remain.

Appendix

Me: We have forgotten something, Brother!

Angel: Have we? What?

Me: Our hearers. They have been very patient with us. It seems a little unmannerly to just let them go without a word of appreciation. After all, we did invite them to overhear us.

Angel: I had not forgotten. You have sung to us, little Brother, and now I shall give our friends a song to sing. They may dance it if they wish. They may take parts and perform it. They may do what they will with it. But let them beware. It is an invocation!

Me: And what a man invokes, that he inexorably receives.

Angel: Indeed he does. Our friends, take the poem that follows with our love and our blessing.

Me: Amen.

Appendix

i. Preparation

Men & Spread the dark earth, prepare the dancing ground;
Women Gather the votaries, raise up the standing stones;

Dance to the rhythm of seed-time and harvest,
Dance to the birth, the death and the rebirth,
Dance to the moonlight and dance to the sun,
Dance to the river, the field and the forest;
Dance to the camp-fire and dance to the morning;
Dance to you know not what, dance in the half-light;
Dance for your night to end, dance for the dawning.

Men Brick on brick, and stone on stone,
Build the world in microcosm.
Sacred highway, pillared hall,
Image of you know not what;
Posture, gesture, gyre and dance,
Calling back a memory
Lost, of long-forgotten things.
All your learning and your lore
Dead, and buried with your kings.

The An angel, speaking through the mind of man
Christ Instructs, illuminates and sanctifies;
And many angels, speaking many different tongues,
Weave a rich pattern, coats of many colors,
Carpeting the highway for the King.

Angels Now comes he, sorrowfully, riding on a donkey,
Angels attending, mortal man triumphant,
Fit to be crucified, fearful of the morning,
Riding to the center of the ring.

The Sword in the Sun

Women   See how the waters of this newer flood
Make glad the city of the Most High God;
See New Jerusalem, of all mankind the building,
Each stone a living soul, towers and gates adorning,
Filled with a radiancy, living and eternal,
Long in the building now, coming Revelation,
Last hope of mortal man; comes the Shadow's ending,
City of the mighty King, crowned and throned and reigning,
Manifesting soon on earth; earth and heaven blending.

Men &   Carpet the earth with a pattern of lights;
Women   First light of morning low on the horizon
Dancing the fire-dance; earth, air and water
Lit and transfigured now, bread and wine and
Rushing wind, newborn man foretelling.

Bright shine the dancing lights, shining through
The shadowed earth; rhythm of the dancing feet
Beating out the time for change; dancing, dancing
Round the ring 'till earth and heaven meet.

Women   Embrace the angels, mortal Man
Embrace your own immortals!
Embrace each other, kiss in peace!
And dance about the bread and wine,
And in the rushing, mighty wind
Fan high the flames of fire on earth
Until that subtle alchemy has wrought
And all's made new. And then, O Man!
Embrace the ecstasy your dance has brought.

Appendix

Men Angels, speaking through the mind of man,
Weave a fair rope of many strands;
And mortal man may weave his fallen will
Into their weaving, cut and trim,
And be at once secured and drawn.

Angels This rope is not for climbing.
So, held and holding, man may go
And tread the path of incarnation,
Knowing what no mortals know.

Women Men, redeemed, immortal, dance
With mortal men; both heaven
And earth their dancing ground.

Angels Then comes the King to dance with them,
To tread the measure with them
Of the end of all things, to renew
All things, and bring redemption's cycle
To a close; with mortal man
Found Faithful, and immortal, True.

Men & Come we now to the dancing of it,
Women Dark earth shining in the midst of heaven,
Bright with dancing feet.

Earth, air and water in the fire of heaven
All transfigured in the dancing of it;
Earth and heaven meet

In the dying and the rising,
Dancing in a field of glory,
New-made and complete.

The Sword in the Sun

Appendix

ii. Meditation

An Angel

Hierarch of the human race, tempted, fell;
And every man, abiding in him, fell with him
Into a slow evolving world of patterns strange
And rhythms barbarous; fell from man
To monkey, thence to rise to something less
Than man; suffer birth and suffer death
Uncomprehending, and be born again
To die again, with love locked in the lower man
And fear surrounding. No hope appears
For mortal man; for birth and death
And birth again, no memory remaining,
Fetter the fallen mind; while inner vision stirs
More sluggish still to see an endless cycle of events
Of no significance and nothing in the making.

Women

Hierarch of the human race,
Identified with fallen earth,
A mother-goddess in the muddled
Mind of mortal man, abode
In silence in eternity
In contemplation of despair
Of mortal men; until the greater
Cycle of the world allowed
Her incarnation.

        Then a maid
Was born into a tragic world,
A second Eden to enact;
And through her 'fiat'
Be the womb of Godhead,
Mark the world's salvation.

The Sword in the Sun

Men   Dancing light in shadowed places,
Elemental Spirits move; unfallen
They, with innocence untainted;
Childlike, with the wisdom of the ages.

Angels   Pan, their hierarch, all-transcending
In their world of Light and Joy,
Dances to the Shadow's ending;
Looks in wonderment and sorrow
At his fallen brothers' lot;
Sees no further than the morrow,
All that's past is soon forgot,

All Pan's subjects leave their traces;
The fallen world is full of faces
Which man cannot, will not, see.

The Christ   Archangels, building in the Mind of God
Thrice-holy temples to the throne of Grace,
Yet turn to man to be their priest
And offer there thrice-holy hymns
To the King, the Father of all.

With all the angels of the heavenly host,
Man dances out the redemption of man
And works a sea-change on a troubled earth;
The rushing, mighty wind of Grace
To fan the tongues of flame,
Thrice-holy hymns to the Father of all,
Thrice-holy dancing to the bread and wine,
Thrice-holy people to attend,
Now and for ever, and world without end.

Appendix

Angels Comes the End? Wake we to a blue sky?
Sun's first rays gleaming on the silent waters?
Hill-tops once are islands now, all
In stillness blending.

Sea-change on a troubled earth; air
Is still and brightening now; fire
Once quenched now rises clear, burns
To sorrow's ending.

All are doomed, yet some remain,
To the hilltops clinging;
All are lost, yet all are found,
Each disaster bringing
Death and Life, and Joy unbounded;
All creation singing!

Men The waters empty from the earth,
And all is changed. And Pan,
Unruffled by the fatal flood,
Will reign within a world unchanged;
The world of men gone, utterly,
Beyond recall; the fell Baptism
Of the fallen world confronting Shadow
With his weird. And man and beast
Departed thence, shall come and go,
The Universe their heritage.

What elements are these? What earth
Is this? Waters covering the earth?
And air? And fire? What mortal woe?
No mortal man shall ever know.

**The
Christ**   All's accomplished! Man is gathered in;
Great fishes in a net that cannot break,
Nor will the fisher's boat be lost,
But all is brought to land, and all
Made new.
                    And on the land the Dance
Begins; a newer measure, better tune.

And all are dancers, all theDance,
And all the dancing ground.
All are singers, all are song;
All, the players; all, the play;
All cast, all plot, all audience.
And all are joyful, all are Joy;
All Love, and all are loving;
All Life, all eternity along.

iii. Affirmation.

An
Angel All things are in the Mind of God,
And all are dancers, all are dancing;
And with them, in the center of his Mind
Is God Himself, their dancing master,

All things move to the music of Grace,
And all are singing, all are song;
And with them, as their central theme,
Is God the Son to sing with them.

All things move to the Rhythm of Love,
And each his own, unique in all eternity;
And with them, beating the time for all,
The Holy Spirit, their Life, their Animation.

All things abide in the Silence of Heaven:
The Silence is the harmony of all
Their song, the stillness is their rhythm;
And all of them, in Love, shall ever abide.

Men A child of Light fell into darkness
And passed beyond the bounds of being,
Remaining but a consciousness, a memory
Of Light, a restless striving for a place
In which to be. This earth, a jewel
In the crown of God, was clutched
And plunged in darkness. Man, fallen,
Fell therein, and made reluctant welcome
For a darkness darker than his own.

The Sword in the Sun

The darkness, now identified with earth,
Began to build and realize its memory.
A parody of heaven then appeared;
A hierarchy of shadows sought to reign,
Born out of torment, clothed in filth
And reared upright in rottenness.
So Satan strove to make a being for himself,
A universe in which he could abide;
His torment and his nothingness to hide.

Now he is lost, and penned
Within the very center of the earth,
His torrent magnified, his time
Run out. The thought-forms of his tortured mind
Rage fiercer, clutching at the psychic bars
Of his self-chosen prison.
About him drift in limbo conscious souls,
Identified with evil, yet from him
And from each other, wholly separate.

The time grows short, the sand has almost run
Out in the hour-glass of God. Begun
The cycle of redemption, turned and turning clear;
The cycle's end, the End of all, is near.

***The
Christ***
    Secure within a sphere of Light, O Man!
    Abide in peace and knowledge of my Love.

The spear which pierced my side shall run you through
And make of you a reed through which my Grace shall blow.

The Serpent-tongue of flame shall rise in you
And make you fit oblation for my mysteries.

Appendix

A Chalice shall you be, a Holy Grail
All emptied and receptive to my filling.

The tide of Light shall rise about you like a Flood,
And with its shining you shall be identified.

A table round, and there, a place for you
To come and go at will in Contemplation

An upper room, symbolic of the world redeemed
In which you shall abide in your redemption

A lamp is there for you to light your way;
I AM your Way, your Light, your Destination.

A winding stair is there for you to climb;
It is a symbol of your own true self,

And climbing, 'though you cannot see,
The mist, the darkness, is my Radiancy.

Women The dance about the Bread and Wine
Is microcosm of the greater Dance
Which is the sum of all that is.

Here dance together mortal men,
Immortals, and the angels too;
With Godhead in the midst of them.

Men bring Him bread and bring Him wine,
With each He is identified,
And with the dancers too.

The Sword in the Sun

The change on earth this dance has wrought
Cannot by mortal man be seen,
Nor can the battles that are fought;
Yet Peace reigns where the strife has been.

The dance about the Bread and Wine
Is anchored to a fallen earth
By mortal men. It is not they
Who labor in the heat of Day
To bring the world redeemed to birth,

But angels and immortal men
Who sing and stoke that dance's fire,
And bring all men into that flame,
Each known, each loved, each called by name;
Until each one is born again
By water and their soul's desire.

The dance about the Bread and Wine
Has worked a sea-change on the shadowed earth,
And as that dance shall seem to die
So shall that change accomplished be;
The earth shall quake, the very sky
Shall fall, all perish to a birth,
New made now, all, for all eternity.

Angels   He is! Because He is, we are
And shall abide in Him always.
O Man! The Bride for such a Bridegroom!
Queen for such a mighty King!
The Universe is made for such a wedding,

Appendix

And everything that is in Him shall sing.

Shall Shadow sing again at that great shining?

Shall souls in limbo turn in ecstasy?
All things are possible, who can say?
For these the Universe shall pray.

iv. Intercession.

The
Christ

The Father, introspective, sets his mental stage
And sees himself upon it; looks for fellow actors
To play the drama of his own eternal Mind,
And looking, sees; and seeing is creation.
The Son of God creates the sons of God;
Archangels mighty who shall build the stage,
Erect the theater, set to dance with him,
And so the Dance begins.

An
Angel

Archangels build the stage, the Son creates the cast;
And Angels in their myriads appear to dance
And build an endless Universe. Within this world
Of shapes and forms, inhabitant and priest is Man!
Created and responsible, below the Angels
Dwelling; a lens through which the light of Grace may shine.

Men

The worlds within this world appear;
Each world is peopled with its living race
Of Elemental Spirits in the shape of man.
Each world a hierarch, every earth a Pan
Receives, to dwell transcendent in his realm
And immanent within its every place.

Women

For every Pan, his people live,
Created for him by the Son;
And after them more living things
Enshrined, on earth, in vegetation.

More creatures yet! The earth itself
Presents to God a living face;

Appendix

Each Element a vital thing,
Each rock and stone a living race.

Angels   And then man fell! A son of God
Was overcome by beauty and was lost;
Turning to the living thing, forgot
The Life Himself. Embracing Man,
He fell;

          and Love threw out a net
Of brute creation into which Man came
Lest he be lost, and working out his fate,
Remain, 'till rescued, 'till restored his name.

An Angel   Embrace, O Man, the rescue wrought,
And dive beneath the changing flood;

Men& Women   Have mercy.

An Angel   Then risen, lead the Risen Life
Which is, and ever is to come.

Men& Women   Have Mercy

An Angel   Know mercy is for ever yours
To know, abide in, and impart;

Men& Women   Have mercy.

An Angel   Restored forever to a place
New-made, creation's very heart;

Men& Women   Have mercy.

The Sword in the Sun

An Angel
Now co-eternal with the Son,
Your Dance is ended; now begun!

Men & Women
Have mercy.

Men
Lord, brute creation, made for me
A refuge; may it rescued be?

Women
Have mercy.

Men
The birds, the creatures of the sea,
The beasts; may they all rescued be?

Women
Have mercy.

Men & Women
That son of God who fell with me
And is not; may he rescued be?

Angels
Have mercy.

The Christ
All brute creation shall be blessed
And, all made new, my Face shall see
For love of Man, his food and rest;
And he who fell with Man's integrity,
Through prayer of Man alone, may rescued be.

v. Oblation.

Men   In union with the Risen Lord
I lay myself before him; no
Gift I bring, no offering make,
No reparation for my former wrongs;
Myself alone I give, whole and entire,
Betokened in this Bread and Wine,

Women   I can give nothing, who am wholly given
Life and being, and a restoration
To life fuller, life more blessed
By far than that from which I fell.
All my thanksgiving, my desire,
Betokened in this Bread and Wine.

**Men &
Women**   What I cannot give, do thou receive
Into a union with thy blessed giving;
And with myself I give my intercession
Into a union with thy priestly prayer,
To cast into that purifying fire
Betokened in this Bread and Wine,

Angels   And now, O Man! Our Brother! we shall dance with you
The microcosm of that greater Dance which swings
Across the Mind of God. The changing wind of Grace
Shall blow, and all things, O Man! all things shall be changed.

**The
Christ**   The Dance is danced, its cycle nearly done;
Come dance, O Man! and dance with me,
And you shall surely see that work begun
Long since, accomplished in felicity.

The Sword in the Sun

Man   I see myself, my triune self,
An image of my Maker,
Once more in integration, clear
Of shadow and released from fear
A freedom I have never known
Is mine; I move between the planes
Of Being on love's errands. Dear
To me the Light of grace and dear,
And dear, and dearer still His Throne.

vi. Consecration.

*The
Christ*

The Dance is danced! About me turn
Angels and men in adoration,
While all creation sings. I take
These tokens, bread and wine;
With me they are identified,
For thus I will, and it is so:

The tale of things is nearly told,
The cycle of Redemption run;
And when the wheel has fully turned,
Then shall Man wake and see full clear
In these same flames in which the world is burned,
I AM, and the new world is begun.

*Angels,
Men &
Women*

So dance we all to generate that flame,
Fanned to its highest by the Wind of Grace,
That shall burn up the mighty flood
And give new earth a kinder face;
Dance to the Body; dance, the Blood!
New Life for man, new rhythm and new Name!

vii. Consummation.

Men &
Women   We who answer to the Cherubim
And sing with them
Thrice-holy songs
To the giver of Life,
The ever-blessed Trinity,
Now lay aside
All the sorrows
And cares of this life.

For now we receive the King of All:
In company with the heavenly host —

Angels   Angels upon angels,
Angels upon angels —

Angels,
Men &
Women   Alleluia!
Alleluia!
Alleluia!

✠   ✠   ✠

For information on additional titles, write:

SUN CHALICE BOOKS
PO Box 9703
Albuquerque, New Mexico
USA 87119